BRAND

MEDIA

STRATEGY

BRAND
MEDIA
STRATEGY

INTEGRATED COMMUNICATIONS
PLANNING IN THE DIGITAL ERA

ANTONY YOUNG

palgrave
macmillan

BRAND MEDIA STRATEGY

First published in 2010 by PALGRAVE MACMILLAN® in the U.S.—a
division of St. Martin's Press LLC, 175 Fifth Avenue, New York, NY 10010.

Where this book is distributed in the UK, Europe and the rest of the world, this is
by Palgrave Macmillan, a division of Macmillan Publishers Limited, registered in
England, company number 785998, of Houndmills, Basingstoke, Hampshire
RG21 6XS.

Palgrave Macmillan is the global academic imprint of the above companies and
has companies and representatives throughout the world.

Palgrave® and Macmillan® are registered trademarks in the United States, the
United Kingdom, Europe and other countries.

ISBN: 978-0-230-10474-7

Library of Congress Cataloging-in-Publication Data

Young, Antony, 1964–
    Brand media strategy : integrated communications planning in the digital era /
Antony Young.
        p. cm.
    Includes bibliographical references and index.
    ISBN 978-0-230-10474-7 (hardback)
    1. Branding (Marketing)   2. Internet marketing.   3. Social media.
I. Title.
HF5415.1255.Y68   2010
658.8'27—dc22
                                                                                    2010025259

A catalogue record of the book is available from the British Library.

Figures by Antonette Maysonet.

Design by Letra Libre, Inc.

First edition: January 2011

10   9   8   7   6   5   4

Printed in the United States of America.

This book is dedicated to
the amazing planning, buying and
digital people at Optimedia US,
from whom I draw inspiration every day.

CONTENTS

ACKNOWLEDGMENTS

Everything I know about this business has come from the people I've met or worked with. Industry thought leaders, figures in the agency world, clients I've worked with, media and business partners and of course my remarkable colleagues at Optimedia US and ZenithOptimedia Worldwide.

I wanted to particularly thank the planning brain trust at Optimedia US, who over the past four years have helped evolve our agency's thinking behind OPEN and torture test many of the Brand Media Strategy concepts in this book. In particular, I want to acknowledge Keith Mackay, Susan Eberhart, Chris Pyne, Vijay Rao, Tom Scott, Greg Kahn and James Shoreland.

Over the years, I have been very fortunate to work with some outstanding communications planning talent at ZenithOptimedia Worldwide, especially Frank Harrison, Derek Morris, Gerry Boyle, Guy Abrahams and David Benson. They unknowingly or directly have contributed to this book through conversations and debates on planning.

Great clients are usually behind great work. Many past and present clients have pushed and challenged me personally to think, act and alter my approach to developing their media communications.

Special thanks to Claire Atkinson for her invaluable perspective and contribution to this book.

I'd also like to thank Antonette Maysonet for creating the figures for *Brand Media Strategy* and Tate Evans for aiding and abetting this book project. Nora Scullin has over the past few years helped me craft my brand media strategy analyses for *Advertising Age* and has my gratitude. My thanks to Belle Lenz and Alysha Walker at DiGennaro Communications for their helpful advice.

Thanks also to Ann Marie Kerwin, Nat Ives and Abbey Klaassen at *Advertising Age* and to Jonah Bloom, its former editor and now chief executive officer at Breaking Media, for allowing me to write about brand media strategy each month. And to David Klein and Cynthia Manson for bringing this opportunity to write an entire book on it!

Of course, this book would not have been as good as it is without the ingenious input of Laurie Harting, executive editor at Palgrave Macmillan.

Finally, to Nancy, for her encouragement and tolerance in allowing me to selfishly bring this book to fruition.

Antony Young
December 2010

FOREWORD

The hit television series *Mad Men* captured the collective imagination of millions of viewers by depicting a romantic period in the history of the American advertising industry. What fans might fail to recognize is that the pervasive drinking, smoking and office romances might have been facilitated by the relative simplicity of the marketing craft in the 1960s. In "the golden age of advertising," big ideas inspired extravagantly produced television commercials that would ultimately air on a handful of networks. Print, radio and outdoor ads played a supporting role. Full stop.

Antony Young entered the world of advertising long after the *Mad Men* era but early enough to witness the profound changes that have rocked the marketing industry in recent years. The twenty-first century ushered in a new paradigm—enabled by consumer choice, exploding technology and proliferating media—and in the process totally redefined the way marketers understand, find, reach and engage their customers. As someone who started his career at Saatchi & Saatchi and rose to lead Optimedia—one of the world's most successful marketing and media agencies—Antony has helped such giants as Sony, Coca-Cola, McDonald's, Nokia, Procter & Gamble and Toyota navigate the chaotic landscape of consumer-brand connection.

In *Brand Media Strategy* Antony parlays nearly twenty-five years of industry experience and human observation into a veritable instruction manual for connecting brand messages to people when and where they are most receptive. Full of practical advice and case studies, the book is a must-read for every industry planner and an illuminating education for anyone who seeks to decipher communications planning in a digital world.

To put the new world order into perspective, consider Nike, which spent $90 million in 1990, predominantly on television advertising. By 2006 the athletic shoe giant was spending $678 million on advertising, and 67 percent of that budget went to online and other digital media.

Thanks to Google, Facebook, YouTube, smart phones, mobile internet and countless place-based opportunities, the path to the passionate for a marketer is complex and convoluted. The mass audience has shattered into a million distinct communities. And while the consumer population is re-amassing, it is doing so according to unique affinities and personal preferences for products, gadgets, content, information, entertainment and so on. Consumers spend nine hours a day engaging with media, and all messages are opt in—or out.

All of these realities contribute to what we call "the blur" of the marketing landscape. *Brand Media Strategy* is an industry application—a GPS if you will—that guides practitioners as they navigate that blur for clients.

Jack Klues
Chief Executive Officer, VivaKi
Publicis Groupe, Directoire
December 2010

INTRODUCTION

I n the first decade of the new millennium a digital revolution swept into the midtown headquarters of New York's media moguls and snapped all the golden rules. Upending business models and the role of mass media itself, that revolution has also engulfed Madison Avenue. The ongoing turmoil brought with it an invigorating tumult of fresh ideas, inspiration and innovation in the marketing and promotion of brands.

Brand Media Strategy is a handbook to help guide the reader in a world where few rules remain. It sets out to help marketing and ad executives turn those exhilarating conference room a-ha moments into winning real-world executions. This book offers strategies that will withstand the turbulence of the ever changing digitally enhanced media communications age.

During the last decade two companies in particular, Google and Facebook, have altered the face of mass marketing. In late 2000, Google unleashed a product called AdWords that handed marketers the ability to capture consumers much further down the purchase funnel. With AdWords, marketers could bypass traditional mass media strategies (in television, radio and print) and directly target people searching for details of a specific service or product. It gave the marketer unprecedented visibility and accountability into advertising as a medium.

Just three years later Facebook founder Mark Zuckerberg and some friends from Harvard University created a force in personal communication that has entranced the world and even dethroned Google as the most visited website in the United States. While the site has yet to figure out a way to unlock major ad dollars, it has had a wide effect on how we think about addressing online communities. Facebook also created a system for disseminating brand preferences that zap back and forth between friends and acquaintances from New York to Nepal. Whoever thought of declaring they were a "fan of Nutella" to their network of friends before Facebook arrived? Facebook's most significant impact on media planning can be summed up with the most persuasive phrase in marketing: word of mouth.

These two ventures have been followed by others, but the power and precedence of Google and Facebook are unrivalled and have shaken the advertising and media professions to their core, forcing a reappraisal of how brands employ media to promote themselves. Marketers and their agencies are scrambling to adapt existing skills and reinvent new ones to take advantage of these major shifts. Digital expertise has moved to the center of planning. It is no longer the icing on the cake.

This book is not about digital media itself but about its impact. Marketing is now as focused on microtargeting as it is on mass media, on response as it is on branding, on earned media as it is on paid media. The lines have blurred across all traditional borders. Google and its band of Silicon Valley engineers, and those Facebook classmates, have crashed the party and changed the media ecology.

Yet over 85 percent of advertising is still invested in the so-called traditional media channels. The owners of television, radio, out-of-home and print media aren't taking all this change lying down. They are evolving as technology plays a more prominent role in creating content for consumers accessing it, not just from television or print, but from gaming devices, smart phones and tablet devices.

Think about how online video sites such as Hulu, owned by News Corporation, NBC Universal and Disney have given marketers the ability to craft campaigns that cross from television to PC and reach viewers wherever they consume media products. Think about how a tweet, a Facebook message and an email from an unknown Illinois senator affected the outcome of an American presidential election.

The rules of engagement have changed. Digital and data have formed powerful bedfellows. And this has been transformational for marketers. The conventions of media planning and buying are being overhauled, and the bar for measuring effectiveness is so much higher than before.

The most progressive marketers tap into new media as well as leverage new ways of dealing with all media channels to win in the marketplace. This book will give you the road map and the compass to develop strategies that work for brands big and small.

A variety of titles already offer instruction and guidelines for advertising media planning, branding and digital marketing. This book is different. It is for the planner who wants to navigate the new media landscape to develop a Brand Media Strategy through communications planning.

Brand Media Strategy shares dozens of case studies that delve deep into planning approaches, including an in-depth discussion of how President Barack Obama used social media to win over voters. We illustrate how Homer Simpson engaged fans to pay to see the *Simpsons* movie in record numbers, when they could see the family on television every week for free. We reveal what went into Denny's television and online campaign that got two million people into their restaurants in a single day. And we share some of the strategic thinking behind Unilever's integrated communication programs for Dove and Axe.

Brand Media Strategy shows you how brands navigate today's media setting by being more calculated and creative. Finally, it provides both marketer and agency the resources to help teams move beyond tactics to craft strategies that ensure brand media communications drives the desire for top-line growth.

Above all, this book is about standing out and being outstanding.

WHY WRITE THIS BOOK?

I've written this book with three main ideas in mind. First, *Brand Media Strategy* deals with the important area of communications planning. Rather than being about how communications for each individual medium is planned, it is about how to develop a strategic and holistic plan that drives brand marketing across platforms. This book complements existing branding, digital and media planning titles.

Brand Media Strategy focuses on what works and what doesn't and how to make effectiveness central to marketers' media programs. It tackles how to embrace all media touch points, from the traditional to the experiential, digital and word of mouth. It also provides a framework and tools for planning these strategies. This book explores methods for agencies and brands to connect communications planning to the creative process.

Second, this book is based on what the media looks like today. It is not an updated edition of an established best media practices title that has sought to add in digital. I look at how the best brands are using media today to be more effective in this more accountable, interactive world.

The latest developments in media, notably in the digital space, have redefined the media landscape and reinvented established advertising practices. This book is not intended to be a history lesson; it is a snapshot of today's ever changing media world and a manual for how brands can best engage with it. It is filled with dozens of very current cases.

This book strongly advocates that digital cannot be a separate function or an adjunct to communications planning. It is in fact one of the most powerful channels and levers for brand communications, one that is integral and often central to *every* media campaign. In the United Kingdom digital advertising spending today exceeds that of television. In the United States, digital media will represent a thirty-billion-dollar advertising market by 2012.[1]

I wrote this book in the midst of the harshest recession since the Great Depression. Accountability and effectiveness are front and center as never before and have become staples for brand marketing communications. Marketers who succeed in this environment will continue to prosper when the economy improves because of what they've learned now. The media that flourishes and innovates in this environment will be the media that survives in the long haul.

Lastly, I've written this book to assist people who are responsible for developing Brand Media Strategies. If you are an agency planner or buyer, you have witnessed some incredible changes in your craft. You're constantly challenged to question established practices, go into new places and be a pioneer in communications. Media's role has stretched beyond its traditional boundaries. There are so many more options and new technologies to consider. You are in one of the most exciting industries I know of, and staying on top of it as it changes and learning new skills are two of the toughest but most essential parts of your job.

This book is also for those in brand management and media management, the people responsible for allocating and managing marketing communication budgets. You don't have to know the ins and outs of media planning and buying, but it's important for you to own the strategy. Media represents an important part of the marketing mix. Ultimately, you are accountable for your decisions, not the agency. This book helps you direct and manage your agency's output.

CHAPTER 1

GOOGLE AND FACEBOOK

HOW THEY'RE CHANGING THE GAME

G oogle and Facebook and a host of other digital media have disrupted the marketing communications profession. The two companies, each in its own unique way, have changed the game. While it is tempting to dismiss popular online fads, the impact of Google and Facebook goes way beyond their respective numbers of visitors or valuations. They have reshaped mass communications globally and opened up opportunities for marketers to execute more accountable, influential and multidimensional campaigns.

Branding has been the foundation of the advertising industry for a century. Broadcast and print advertising's forte was in growing brand awareness and building a brand. In some respects, digital media has set higher standards, in effect repositioning the industry's perspective of established media, because digital media enables consumer response measurement. Tracking and optimization tools for online media provide granular and near real-time response to creative material, which allows not just a higher degree of accountability but more sophistication in influencing buyer behavior.

Digital media also provides a level of interactivity that by its very nature enables a more personalized experience. Users are able to get information how and when they want it. The internet has become the information medium of choice and a significant factor in influencing purchase decisions. For marketers, digital media provides insight into how to reach customers and convert interest into intent to purchase.

The peer-to-peer connectivity of social media needs to become central to every marketer's thinking. Will we soon take product recommendations from our ten closest friends on Facebook or from a blog found on Google? Marketers are preparing for these possibilities. According to comScore/Kelsey Group research, nearly one in four internet users looked at online reviews before selecting a restaurant or hotel or legal, travel, medical, automotive or home services.[1] Another survey reveals that, among teens, 39 percent of word of mouth about a brand happens online via text, email, instant messaging, chats and blogs.[2]

Knowing the digital media space is vital to getting the most out of advertising. Let's take a brief look at the two companies.

GOOGLE: THE MAGIC, THE LOGIC

For decades, advertising has been about creativity, art and emotional connections. And then about a decade ago, Google shook things up, bringing with it an advertising era based on math, reason and logic. Google offered to solve the age-old conundrums of marketers: waste and accountability. What marketer wouldn't want solutions to both?

Google helped advertisers by delivering the ability to directly target consumers at the moment they're looking for a product or service. Google serves up an ad on its search site and elsewhere at the precise point in time that people are researching a potential purchase or, even better, ready to buy online. Quite simply, Google's AdWords program has revolutionized the way companies big and small advertise.

One has only to look at Google's financials to see the extent of its success. According to one estimate, AdWords accounts for 95 percent of Google's profit. Full-year profit at Google was $6.5 billion in 2009, while revenue was $23.65 billion. By comparison, Time Warner's entire Time Inc.

division, which publishes titles as large as *People* and *InStyle,* reported profits of $246 million in 2009.

Google's ability to serve as a conduit for sellers looking for customers has created billions of dollars in profitability, and few think Google's potential is anywhere near fulfilled, such is its lock on our collective consciousness. "Google and its competitors have created the first application to leverage the database of intentions in a commercial manner: paid search," writes John Battelle in *The Search: How Google and Its Rivals Rewrote the Rules of Business and Transformed Our Culture.*[3] Battelle came up with the phrase "the database of intentions" to convey the power Google holds in knowing what we're all searching for, whether it's boots, books, doctors or divorces. Google's advantage comes in matching advertisers to all those searches for information. What ads web users see depends on a variety of factors, but the most important one is the ads' relevance to the initial search phrase. "It is a very efficient marketing program," says former Gateway online strategist Antonella Pisani. "You are capturing people while they are interested."[4]

For an example of AdWords' effectiveness, take Paul Bond Boots, an Arizona-based family-owned business that sells cowboy boots. When asked, "How good of a program is Google AdWords for small business?" one of the company executives said, "In my opinion it would be indispensable at a time like this."[5] In 2009, the company's ad showed up on the right in the sponsored links section when "cowboy boots" was typed in the search box. But Google AdWords isn't a media sales tool for just the Paul Bonds of this world. Fortune 100 companies such as CitiGroup, IBM and even Google competitor Microsoft rely on Google's utility and targetability for their commercial success. It's hard to imagine Amazon as the company it is today without Google AdWords.

The change that Google has wrought on advertising cannot be overstated. It forced a paradigm shift for advertisers, moving their decision making away from targeting demographics and mass audiences to connecting with individuals in a much more relevant way. As a result marketers have seen wastage significantly reduced. Since AdWords' cost is based on an auction model connected to the price and effectiveness of the advertising, the onus is on the advertiser to develop more effective copy. Google's brilliance is that advertisers can see whether a coupon or a free recipe is more effective. And even better, advertisers can adjust their plan almost instantaneously without significant additional costs, in contrast to making ad changes in traditional media, which is slow and expensive.

Advertisers can't buy their way to the top—the ads have to be relevant to the people typing the search term, and Google ranks the site they are directed to by its quality. And that is a critical point for a marketing strategy—how well do you know customers and how well are you targeting them with the message *they* want to hear. How much marketers pay for their ads to be clicked on is decided by factors that Google—not the advertiser—controls. Yet Google has democratized advertising, making it accessible to small advertisers and taking away the clout and scale enjoyed by bigger fish.

Ken Auletta in his book *Googled: The End of the World as We Know It* observed that Google believes it is helping to shape a new and better media world by making the buying of advertising more accountable and transparent. In Google's view, the company serves consumers by offering advertising as information. And by offering a bidding system based on rewarding the more responsive ads it is helping to improve advertising performance.[6]

Google's largest impact on the media business as a whole has been to force it to compare its conventional metrics with sophisticated internet data. In an attempt to stem the flow of dollars to more accountable media, television networks agreed to move from program ratings—the currency of the industry since television ad buying began—to commercial break ratings, which made it possible to estimate how many people were viewing a particular commercial. Newspaper executives only provide circulation figures; whereas online advertisers know exactly who's reading what story when readers connect digitally.

What's more, consumers' appetite for online searches appears to be growing. Worldwide, those aged fifteen or older conducted 131 billion searches in 2009—a 46 percent jump on the previous year's number, according to comScore. Google's share of that figure in the United States alone was 65.6 percent.[7]

Google has highlighted the undeniable fact that the established advertising business was built around a soft measurement—say, ratings or readers or impressions. The increased transparency of online advertising's direct impact on sales and leads is pushing other media to do better. Our clients will no longer accept "estimated measures" of success when digital media provides them with hard data that can be tied directly to results.

Interestingly, the search giant isn't known for doing its own brand advertising very often, but it does reach out to the ad community through the odd print ad. One such ad, figure 1.1 (see page 12), explains in very simple terms four ways the company can help marketers. In many ways that copy reflects this new era of advertising accountability that Google champions.

Google isn't resting on its search laurels. Google entered the ad network business with AdSense in 2005. AdSense offers advertisers the opportunity to serve relevant display ads—text, image or video—based on content and user and behavioral data. Their bet on mobile devices is manifested in the Android operating system and an array of mobile applications. Speaking at Atmosphere, Google's conference for chief information officers, Google's chief executive officer Eric Schmidt signaled the company's focus on that platform when he said, "Mobile will ultimately be the way you provision most of your services. The way I like to put it is the answer should always be mobile first. You should always put your best team and your best app on your mobile app."[8] During the week of the 2010 television upfronts, Google launched Google TV, which attempts to make live television and the Internet into a seamless experience for viewers. The most interesting feature of Google TV is that, by essentially treating websites as television channels, viewers will have access to a virtually unlimited number of content choices on a single display, their television set.

FACEBOOK'S INFLUENCE OF HALF A BILLION FRIENDS

The number of social media sites is exploding, and usage is up in almost every dimension—as good a reason as any for marketers to take note. And here's the clincher: Facebook is now the biggest website in the world.

FIGURE 1.1

4 ways our logic can help you work your magic.

1.

KNOW WHAT YOU DON'T KNOW

Knowing trumps guessing every time. Use our free tools to know what consumers are talking about, looking for, engaging with, and visiting. Take our Insights for Search tool. You can discover regional search patterns and trends, then take advantage of them by adapting your messages in key markets. Instead of best guesses, you've now got an informed strategy.
Also consider: Google Ad Planner, Google Analytics, Google Alerts

2.

AMPLIFY YOUR CREATIVITY

If your creativity knows no bounds, neither should your creative. Use our digital tools to explore possibilities and breathe more life into your campaigns. Take DoubleClick Studio. You can create captivating, interactive rich media ads using simple, drag-and-drop, pre-made components. Your inspiration now has a lot more opportunity to inspire.
Also consider: iGoogle Gadgets, YouTube InVideo ads, Ad Creation Marketplace for Google TV Ads

3.

BUY MEDIA THAT MATTERS

Spellbinding creative will fall flat if your message never connects. Use our advertising solutions to reach the right customers: Yours. Take Placement Targeting on the Google Content Network. You can zero in on your audience by easily selecting specific ad placements—entire sites, sections of sites, or even particular spots on particular pages. You've now created meaningful connections, and are paying only what they're worth to you.
Also consider: Search, display, TV, and mobile advertising, all via Google AdWords

4.

GET RESULTS, THEN GET BETTER RESULTS

As you work your magic, you'll want to know how well it's working. Use our free reporting and optimization tools to learn what's working, what's not, and what'll work better. Take Custom Reports in Google Analytics. You can quickly create tailored views of the website metrics, making it easy to review and act on the information important to you. With all of these tricks up your sleeve, now you're ready to go make more magic. Logically.
Also consider: AdWords Report Center, Website Optimizer, YouTube Insight

Visit www.google.com/advertisers to learn how these and other Google solutions can help you work your magic.

Google

Launched by Mark Zuckerberg in 2004 from his Harvard University dorm, Facebook began life as a site to help fellow students share videos and messages rather than emailing them or uploading them to clunky sites. Facebook's simple interface, rather like Google's simple home page, is one reason its popularity has leapfrogged other sites such as MySpace. In 2010 Facebook had over 500 million users. The website claims that the average user has 130 friends.

Perhaps the most stunning statistic is time spent on Facebook. Web users are spending much more time connecting with their groups. According to Nielsen figures for December 2009—a much-watched period since people spend more time in December connecting with friends and family and doing online shopping than any other month—time spent on social networking sites rose 86 percent compared with the previous year. On December 25 Facebook overtook Google as the top site in terms of traffic for the first time.[9] According to Facebook, half of their active users log in to the site every day.

While Facebook's advertising revenue has been limited thus far, its impact on the marketing business has been huge. Suddenly the power of word of mouth, networks and small groups can become magnified globally, as we saw with candidate Obama's message of hope and his call to action.

When a new disaster strikes in the world, social media sites, such as Facebook and Twitter, are increasingly the places that people turn to first, to find out what happened from friends or witnesses reporting before the news media. The New York–based *Haitian Times* wrote in January 19, 2010, that "the use of social networks as a major way of communications is a first for Haitians, who have traditionally relied on radio and word of mouth as the best source of information."[10]

David Kirkpatrick writes that Zuckerberg and others at Facebook "believe [that] more visibility makes us better people. Some claim, for example, that because of Facebook, young people today have a harder time cheating on their boyfriends or girlfriends. They also say that more transparency should make for a more tolerant society in which people eventually accept that everybody sometimes does bad or embarrassing things."[11] This idea has migrated to brands and how people respond positively to the transparency that social media encourages. In a world where consumers are becoming more cynical and dismissive of corporate-controlled brand messaging, Facebook represents the media of the everyday person. Hence marketers and their agencies are trying to tap into the Facebook effect. They're trying to create Facebook brands built out from within the Facebook community and thus personally relevant in this more transparent and authentic world.

Here's a handful of reasons why marketers need to know about Facebook and other social media networks:

- They provide a rich data mine of people's current interests, for example, a book or movie. It's a global focus group.
- They enable marketers to see what's working and what's not and put more money behind those products and services gaining most positive mentions (see the Coca-Cola brand page on www.facebook .com/cocacola).
- Facebook and others might one day replace email as a simple form of messaging.
- Social media sites are portable and can be accessed from a smart phone, enabling marketers to connect 24/7 and also serve up messages based on the viewer's location.
- "Like" pages allow users to tell their friends of their support for certain brands.
- Facebook gives advertisers the ability to target; Facebook users share their geography, birthday, gender, relationship status, age and education level.
- The early internet advertising strategy of driving traffic to a corporate site has been superseded by the strategy of brands living on sites that users enjoy spending time on.

The smartest brands are on Facebook and doing their utmost—building brand pages, building traffic for those pages and promoting their products in entertaining ways. "Companies cannot traverse the web quick enough.

They need to create these unpaid armies of customers to do this on their behalf," claims Jeremiah Owyang, a partner with Altimeter Group.[12]

One of the most popular brand sites is Coca-Cola's, built not by the company but by true brand evangelists. The company's 7.6 million fans post their love of the drink alongside photos of their Coke merchandise collections.[13] Similarly, Starbucks has 10.3 million fans sharing their enjoyment of caramel lattes in a sentence or posting videos of their kids enjoying the cafés.[14] The page has an option for suggesting a friend so you can share your love of a product. Best Buy, another company with a huge Facebook presence, has built a page that doesn't promote products; rather, it lets visitors get feedback about products from other Facebook friends and provides the marketer with feedback from customers. The site also has a Shop and Share feature.

As social media continues to evolve, new sites and platforms will arise and be the first to catch the next wave. But Google and Facebook are the first significant players to have broken through and influenced everyone in our business. It won't ever be the same.

CHAPTER 2

THE NEW MEDIA PLAYBOOK

A NEW SET OF RULES FOR
A NEW MEDIA WORLD

In the old world of top-down, one-way communication, a company told you what it wanted you to hear, and you had the choice to take it or leave it. In the new digital world of transparency and ready access to amazing quantities of detailed information on just about everything, companies will be held much more to account.

—Simon Clift, former global chief marketing officer,
Unilever

As a kid growing up, I remember discarding my Larry Bird Converse sneakers for the latest set of Nikes. I really did think they made me jump higher and shoot the basketball better. I would later learn when I entered the ad business that it was all about branding.

Nike is one brand that has wisely used its marketing to remain relevant. It has transformed its Brand Media Strategy from the golden age of mass advertising to one that takes full advantage of the Google and Facebook era.

Back in the eighties and nineties Nike's ad campaigns were the gold standard of the marketing community. Michael Jordan was the face of the brand for youngsters, whether they lived in an inner city or a leafy suburb.

The sneaker brand aired its first national television spot in 1982. By 1988 Nike launched that unforgettable tagline "Just do it," which became an *Advertising Age* top-five slogan of the twentieth century. The marketing helped propel the company to a 23 percent share of the athletic shoe market.[1]

Fast-forward twenty years and Nike's strategy looks very different. In 2006 Nike spent just 33 percent of its $678 million US budget in traditional media, a 55 percent drop from the previous ten years.[2] Now, Nike shows many of its ad spots only on the internet. A two-minute, forty-six-second spot starring soccer player Ronaldinho garnered twenty eight million views on YouTube.[3]

The Nike vice president for global brand marketing, Joaquin Hidalgo, espouses this approach, commenting, "Consumers don't want to be told what's cool. People don't want more products, they want more experiences. . . . Now we put consumers smack dab in the middle of everything we do, placing them in the center and engaging with them is what we like to do. Our consumer is growing up in a different world. One big thing changing in their world is the notion that they are digitally enabled and connected."[4]

For that approach, Nike realized that advertising wouldn't be enough, and the firm began to develop "experiences." The company created an online community for runners when it offered them its Nike+ sensor. The sensor records a runner's activity on an Apple iPod. Runners upload their workout activity to a website and read web logs written by coaches.

Separately, the athletic apparel giant arranged for five coaches and seventeen pacers to lead runs through Central Park three times a week starting from one of Nike's stores in Manhattan. Nike organized the Human Race, a 10K running event in twenty-five cities with eight hundred thousand participants.

Nike released its fourth line of sneakers attached to the NBA star LeBron James, called Nike Air Zoom LeBron IV. The shoe was the sole sponsor of an episode of ESPN's *SportsCenter*, and Nike distributed four hundred thousand DVDs of the making of the shoe and its unique ad campaign, proving that advertising can be seen as entertainment.

The company used a host of fresh media outlets for the sneaker debut, including MTV.com and ESPN.com. The marketing department ran video clips on MTV2 and erected a neon billboard near New York's Madison Square Garden that continuously showed LeBron dunking.

There is no question that what Chris Anderson dubbed the long tail of media (all the small outlets that target tiny audiences that when put together represent a targeted mass) presents tremendous opportunities to a savvy marketer.[5] Nike proved this by using the tail to outmaneuver its rival Adidas during the 2010 soccer World Cup: Leading into the tournament, Nike launched a three-minute video ad called "Write the Future" on its Facebook page. The spot featured famous footballers such as England's Wayne Rooney and Portugal's Cristiano Ronaldo. Fans were encouraged via an online tool to edit the spot. These edited versions competed for votes.

Five weeks after its debut, the online spot had been viewed by over 20 million people. Nike enjoyed twice as much buzz associated with the World Cup than official sponsor Adidas.[6]

Nike has evolved its marketing along with the times, it has employed new forms of advertising on new media channels as they hit critical mass and it has shown just how close to the consumer companies have to be to stay front of mind.

Stefan Olander, global director for brand connections at Nike, says, "We want to find a way to enhance the experience and services, rather than looking for a way to interrupt people from getting to where they want to go."[7] Nike's products continue to be in demand and it remains the world's number-one seller of athletic footwear and apparel.

THE MEDIA WORLD IS EVOLVING FAST

The media business has always shaped how advertising has evolved. The two businesses are intertwined like no others. They feed each other, they support each other and they innovate together. Newspaper publishers created the ad industry, radio aired sponsored programs in its early days and television fueled brand advertising in its golden years. The eighties saw the growth of cable television and the targeting of the MTV generation, while the nineties ushered in the internet and an army of digital agencies and interactive advertising. This led to more sophisticated targeting, better understanding of response and the development of corporate and brand websites along with an unprecedented level of interactivity. At the opening of the 2010s, we see the ad model is shifting yet again, with Google and Facebook leading the way in remaking communications. There's a new agenda and a new media playbook for marketers.

FROM BROADCAST TO BROAD "CATCH"

"Technology is creating new media options faster than most people can assimilate and is causing more multitasking," says Gary Drenik, president of the consumer intelligence firm BIGresearch.[8]

As we get greater internet access, more bandwidth and increased portability of media and content, we have discovered that consumers' appetite for information and entertainment grows geometrically. Linear media is fast giving way to liquid media, in which consumers can move seamlessly from setting to setting. And it is commonplace for people of all ages to consume multiple media—television, internet, newspaper, text messaging and other media—at the same time.

The concept of mass media has shifted. Television's top-rated show twenty years ago, *The Cosby Show*, reached 27 percent of the population; today's *American Idol* reaches less than 9 percent.[9]

We're seeing media's growing long tail. As we consume more media, the existing media channels are fragmenting and new ones are being added. The proliferation of new channels means less viewer time per channel. The explosion of new video and content created by the internet and mobile platforms divides audiences into smaller and smaller segments. Current mass media markets are ephemeral, and revenues per channel will decrease.

We are moving from a world of broadcast to broad "catch." Consumers are harder to reach and creating mass awareness is more complex. In the past, running a concurrent television and newspaper campaign was enough. People would see both. Now viewers may see one, the other or neither. Campaigns need to be multimedia and multichannel, and creative ideas have to travel and make sense in different formats. As many as 60 percent of television viewers go online while they're watching, and websites of magazines and newspapers add video stories daily.[10]

With most media consumed with only partial attention, the impact of advertising decreases. Today, McKinsey estimates that television advertising is only 35 percent as effective as it was in 1990.[11] Clutter is one of the biggest problems for marketers.

targeting?

An implication of this shift is that marketers need more than great creative; they need to have the message appear in the right context. For advertising to reach consumers and not be filtered out, it must be in a relevant place where the consumer will be more likely to engage with the message.

Advertising is bought and sold today in ways dramatically different from the past. Some companies aggregate audiences across multiple distribution channels—such as the online ad networks—and others deliver messages directly to individual users after discerning their attitudinal and consumption patterns.

EVERYONE'S A MEDIA COMPANY

We are witnessing an explosion of media creation across blogs, video and photo sites, social networks and beyond. People's media activities are increasingly focused on participatory channels such as Facebook. In September 2010 there were over 500 million people on Facebook, 145 million on Twitter and 20 million bloggers.

Five years after its launch, YouTube exceeds two billion video views per day. Every minute, people upload twenty-four hours of video content to the video channel owned by Google. Mobile devices have become much more of a social media channel today, with more smart phones sold than PCs.

It's a content jungle out there: personal profiles, Apple's "There's an app for that" product line, the OpenSocial standard and more all vie for consumer attention.

ADVERTISER FILTERING

As a backlash to the ever increasing onslaught of advertising, consumers filter and, even worse, block advertising. Technologies such as TiVo and banner blockers have seen to that. Online print editions have also reduced advertiser intrusiveness.

Research companies are stuffed with data on how much people hate advertising. According to a survey from Sweden's Research International, 22 percent actively avoid advertising in all media. A global media survey from media intelligence firm Synovate found that 67 percent of respondents thought television had too many ads and that roughly 40 percent thought the same of the internet. The study also revealed that more than 80 percent of internet users in Australia, Canada, Spain and the United States actively avoid websites containing "intrusive" advertising.[12]

Consumers overwhelmed with ad messages are, not surprisingly, increasingly selective about what they watch and the advertising messages they trust. Media companies recognize this, and some have developed interesting TiVo-busting solutions. For example, the CW Television Network created content wraps to weave beauty products into small advice spots around the reality show *America's Next Top Model*. Google is testing a system based on choice. Users are asked which ad or advertiser they don't want to see.

THE SPEED AND ACCESSIBILITY OF DATA

Ratings and readership have been the basis for media planning and the currency of media buying for the past fifty years. But marketers today have much more information about media and consumer purchase habits.

Current media measurement is designed for planning campaigns based on the principles of building brands and driving mass awareness. The industry is moving fast toward direct marketing principles that at their heart are about measuring response and gaining more exact return-on-investment numbers.

The accessibility of data, and the speed at which it is available, has made it easier for marketers to evaluate and optimize campaigns with higher precision. Marketers have been able to adjust a campaign as it evolves, fine-tuning efficiency and response. New media-measurement techniques have allowed marketers to test and improve each campaign over time, changing creative, media placement, position and timing.

The digital era has bypassed demographics. Marketers have a clearer picture of a consumer from the content they've viewed. Online data could, for instance, tell a car manufacturer which model consumers looked at on their own site. They could then correlate that with the consumer's zip code (deduced from information the consumer entered on a weather site) and the consumer's tastes (from the consumer's access of sports or fashion sites).

Websites deliver a wealth of response and impact data, for instance, the number of impressions (or views), response or cost per click, number of on-line video views, level of engagement (time on site, number of pages viewed, purchase activity), pass-on of the site to friends and the number of online friends a person has. Marketers can gain insight by measuring the level and intensity of conversations via blogs, Twitter, aggregator Digg.com and social networking sites. This rapid delivery and accessibility of data has created an industry built to track, evaluate and optimize. Marketers adjust their campaigns more speedily now that they know what works and what doesn't.

Stephen DiMarco, chief marketing officer for Boston-based Compete, referring to his company's merging of data with Cannondale's to create a consumer panel with online and offline data, says, "Since we have 'matched' our panel with Cannondale, we can determine what [consumer packaged goods] products our panelists have purchased. This means we can use this information as the basis of our segmentation and then build media plans based on the recency and/or frequency of purchase in a product category like diapers."[13]

A MEDIA MASH-UP

Speaking at an Optimedia client digital off-site in June 2010, VivaKi's chief innovations officer Rishad Tobaccowalla observed, "All analog media are becoming digital. Most digital media are becoming mobile. Most mobile media are becoming analog."

Established media aren't being left out of the picture; they're buying and creating their own new media. The world's oldest advertising medium, the out-of-home (OOH) industry (for example, billboards), is investing heavily in digital OOH networks. In a deal valued at $1.8 billion, CBS acquired CNET Networks, including TV.com, one of YouTube's biggest suppliers. NBC Universal and News Corporation came together to create online video player Hulu. The partners later welcomed the Walt Disney Co. as a participant. Disney also has a close relationship with Apple and was the first to sell its television shows via iTunes.

The business is no longer about buying online versus television versus print. We are witnessing the rise of audiovisual media with advances such as three-dimensional television, interactive television and mobile video. Arguably, iPads and etablets could be the predominant platform for magazines in the future.

Media companies are looking to sell across platforms such as television and the internet, and the media plan will follow that content. The media business was built on delivering large audiences, measured by demographics, and advertisers bought those audiences. Now the media business targets by content, behavior and response. To give an example, the hit comedy *The Office*, broadcast Thursday nights on NBC, is available after the broadcast on the online video site Hulu.com. Fans can also follow a blog written by one of the show's characters, Dwight, and view unedited scenes on their mobile phones. One example of an advertiser taking advantage of a cross-platform approach was Hyundai in Fox's *24*. In addition to advertising in the show, they were the only automotive advertiser to build into the show brand and product placement. They promoted and ran exclusive scenes online for the next week's show. They advertised their association with the show in print and radio. Lastly, they sponsored the *24* episodes on Hulu.

Smart phones are fast becoming the platform of choice for accessing social media applications. Mobile technology has increased the applications' utility and accessibility among users. And mobile technology seems to be meeting very analog needs—ordering pizza, reading magazines, searching for local addresses and accessing directions.

THE ECONOMICS OF ESTABLISHED MEDIA COMPANIES ARE ERODING

All this choice for advertisers is driving down costs. Traditional media outlets are suffering.

In 2009, 369 magazines ceased publishing and 64 print titles were entirely replaced by online editions. Consumers these days want information in real time. Newspapers are losing audience as Generation Y reads print online and classified advertising shifts to the internet. As the cost of producing information becomes too much to bear for major network news departments, Twitter has stepped in, breaking news faster, and for free, thanks to unpaid amateurs on the ground.

At the same time, social media still searches for a revenue model, and mobile advertising is in its infancy. We're seeing a pushback on media, with the likes of News Corporation and the *New York Times*, with its prominent online properties, instituting pay walls on websites.

The chaos is creating opportunities, with media companies wanting to amortize their content and their resources differently. The next few years will see a dramatic shift in how the entire media business is underwritten, whether by the consumer or the advertiser.

THE NEW MEDIA PLAYBOOK

In truth, we've been seeing the mass media age erode for some time. Search engines and social media have just added to the pressure on the gas pedal.

The shift in the media world and with consumers is a double-edged sword for those in the advertising and communications business. We're an industry that thrives on fashion and fads. But the changes I've just outlined have real-world implications for developing and executing Brand Media Strategies. There are eight important implications for the new media playbook.

CREATE INVOLVEMENT AND RELEVANCE, NOT JUST AWARENESS

Advertising has always been about engaging the consumer. In the golden age of mass media, it was all about the creative: the funniest commercial, the most captivating print ad. Now advertising is as much about creating involvement and relevance as grabbing attention.

Since generating awareness is expensive and more difficult to achieve in a fragmented, partial-attention media economy, advertising relies on precision—it's less about the number of people exposed to a message and more about locating the right audience. The notion of advertising interrupting consumers is giving way to a more audience-friendly approach. As consumers filter and avoid advertising, the context of advertising is becoming as important as the content.

In today's market, advertisers are working even harder to put the right message in front of the right target group at the right time to improve the performance of their communications. To give an example, the Volkswagen Polo has been using online video to reach its customers in Europe. VW knows exactly whom it wants to target: a man between the ages of twenty-five and thirty-nine, who "watches soccer matches, checks out the Playboy site and reads *Der Spiegel* magazine."[14] That's a whole lot different from and more specific than the demographic buys of television, targeting men ages eighteen to thirty-four.

Christian Baudis, the European head of Tremor Media, a New York–based advertising network, tells Bloomberg, "We go to them [the client] and say here are 150 sites with video content that is attractive to that target group. Targeted advertising is more efficient. It costs less money to reach the target. That's the beauty of it."[15]

Jeremy Allaire, head of Brightcove, a company that helps manage video content on scores of websites, adds that with online advertising a marketer knows exactly how many people have seen the ad. In contrast to a brand impression on television, he said, "on the Internet, a video ad comes up and it's designed as a call to action for the user and they can click it, taking them to the marketing Web site."[16]

Media technology and its rapid development have increased advertisers' ability to exploit the relevance and context of the messages. But the pursuit of relevant context is not limited to digital media. Major broadcasters are exploring more integrated sponsorships or branded entertainment in program platforms. The win–win is when it works organically for the brand and the program. Print publications are developing smart advertising and editorial programs that offer synergy for brands. And cable television companies are positioned to orchestrate addressable advertising, which the advertising industry sees as the next step for television. Addressable advertising is television's version of online advertising. It targets households with relevant ads based on viewer and household data.

ADOPT DIGITAL PRACTICES AS BEST PRACTICES FOR ALL MEDIA

Marketers and their agencies are finding inspiration in the digital world. Digital agencies tossed a lot of what was wrong with the traditional business and invented new ways to operate. The general advertising industry would be more effective if it adopted the marketing thinking and skills that digital marketers have championed for years.

Brand versus Return on Investment

What's more important, brand or return on investment? Digital marketers have been able to more consistently walk the tightrope between the two. The digital world has owned the return-on-investment mantra. Interactive media has grown in popularity because it can track response, behavior and sales. It establishes metrics at the outset of a campaign and tracks performance against them. Metrics quickly evolved beyond response campaigns to brand campaigns, from basic page views and click-through statistics to engagement and sales-effect metrics. In comparison, analog marketing measures such as ad awareness and brand measures appear soft and often are unrelated to business outcomes.

Integration

The cascading of marketing agency specialists (direct response, media, customer relationship management, design, sponsorship, entertainment marketing, custom publishing, etc.) has the industry debating whether this has led to sacrifice of integration. Digital advertising, with a few exceptions, has built its model on a fully integrated service. Marketers expect digital people to give them a knowledgeable critique of the website, creative, research, brand and media activity and to integrate it all. Imagine having your creative team at an ad agency sitting alongside media and adjusting their TV ads according to response!

Campaign Planning versus Campaign Optimization

Digital marketers tweak marketing communications in real time. If an idea fails, they make adjustments along the way. The new thinking advocated by digital marketers is to constantly test and reapply. This has also led to creating different models and a cost structure for developing creative executions and content.

Cutting Out Advertising Waste

The ability to segment targeting has been around ever since the publishing industry launched special interest titles. The potential to cut waste or narrowly target through niche print or television media and messaging never really got off the ground. We continue to be locked into a media buying currency of cost per thousand demographic audience such as all adults eighteen to forty-nine. We rarely if ever see marketers employ different creative on, say, Syfy versus MTV. But digital marketers have made this happen, and they are getting results.

Participation Media

It was only a few years ago that the internet was being written off as an advertising medium as agencies tried desperately to fit old media logic into the new media environment.

The viral, irreverent campaign of Burger King's subservient chicken in the United States broke new ground by encouraging twelve million viewers to type commands that a man dressed in a chicken suit responded to, to reinforce its "Have it your way" tagline.

Marketers need to incorporate all these kinds of skills and disciplines into their general communications.

LET CONSUMER INSIGHT DRIVE THE MEDIA STRATEGY

Until we take steps to advance our understanding of people we won't be able to enjoy the full benefits of this exciting new age.

—Susan Gianinno, chairman and chief executive officer,

Publicis North America

Media selection is more than just reaching the consumer; it's delivering memorable, interactive and emotional occasions with the brand. The key is planning media from the consumer's perspective. Yet media agency planners are guilty of being media facing instead of consumer facing. In the mass media era, planning was all about measuring audiences and buying media on the basis of the most efficient and best levels of coverage. Awareness has given way to involvement and relevance. Today's strategies need to be driven by communications platforms with insight at the center.

MEDIA NEUTRALITY

If consumer insight drives Brand Media Strategy, then it follows that marketers and their agencies have to be Switzerland when it comes to deciding which media to use. Because influence has become more important than reach, how the hierarchy of media changes depends on the category and brand task. We can't assume television is the lead medium or that digital should drive all campaigns. Brand media dollars are too precious to make such broad statements. Nor can we rely solely on advertising as the primary marketing tool. Marketers have at their disposal paid, earned and owned media, and each brings something to the equation.

This has major implications for marketers' approach to development of their marketing communications. The process for developing advertising needs to start with "Where should we be?" and then move to "How to say it?" rather than the other way around. All touch points help build a brand. Different mixes of marketing channels and media create different outcomes. The role of media and channel selection has become more of a strategic decision by marketers.

MICROMEDIA MAKES WORD-OF-MOUTH MARKETING MORE SCALABLE

Word of mouth has always been the most effective way to market a brand, and it is now more scalable. Micromedia has made it so.

Micromedia is media consumed separately from traditional media, even if traditional media outlets are producing it. Think about all the people who read the *New York Times* financial Dealbook blog but may never pick up the newspaper. Micromedia is a video on YouTube versus E! Entertainment or an iTunes download versus a CD.

Micromedia can be reconstructed and aggregated in many different ways, such as RSS feeds or blog networks or podcasts. Micromedia simultaneously expands the media supply and atomizes it. The size of media products shrinks. More of us are snacking, taking bite-size pieces of media as smart phones and iPods transform downtime into opportunities to catch up on email, share information or watch a webisode. The downside is that less of us are sitting down to the full five-course menu.

Media such as Facebook and Twitter metastasize word of mouth. The benefit for marketers is that all this media activity has made the consumer conversation more widespread. Marketing messages can be spread online, and that's put new vigor behind grassroots media outlets with a closer connection to their readership. Consumers are more likely to believe other individuals than a faceless corporation. Friends and acquaintances are seen as more authentic and transparent.

Even journalists are influenced by social media: 89 percent reported using blogs for their research.[17] Earned media (free media, PR, buzz) needs to become integral to many brand communications. Consumers' participation in media means they are part of the medium and message for brands. In many cases they are willing partners if properly tapped.

SEARCH IS THE LAST MILE OF MARKETING

Online search is now the most important medium in advertising. Coming from a media guy whose career has been made by developing great television, print or OOH campaigns, that's a sweeping statement. But here's why. It's where people start to look for information and filter the information that's out there. It makes the whole experience of looking for products and services so much more personal.

It's certainly the most accountable. Google's model of weighting ads that are more relevant has rubbed off on the advertising world. The more relevant an ad message, the more effective, because the message is then seen as information. No more ad avoiders. And when consumers seek information about products and services, they usually turn to Google or any of the other search engines, such as Bing or Yahoo! Search is second only to browsing in malls as the most influential activity in encouraging purchase, according to a survey by Netpop Research.[18]

No one visits a website home page anymore—they walk in the back door, the page that Google sent them to. Google is the starting point for most consumers who want to find out more about a brand or need help making a decision. It has almost single-handedly replaced the traditional role of print advertising and in-store advice in providing product information.

Any advertising effort then should prioritize the search strategy. Integrating search with an existing effort is a major opportunity. Supporting marketing efforts that are lower in the purchase funnel, when customers are in the information-gathering stage of researching a product or service, will likely improve their efficiency. Search allows marketers to tap into awareness and interest generated by your current advertising.

Search inquiries very often are generated by publicity. When Michelle Obama appeared on Jay Leno's *Tonight Show* and mentioned her outfit was from J. Crew, the retailer leaped on the opportunity, bought the search term "Michelle Obama" and set up a page on JCrew.com that promoted her outfit.

Search exploits one of the most powerful qualities of marketing: relevant messaging. It influences brand decisions and increases brand consideration when prospects are in the market. Search is not just an advertising medium; it is a sales-lead tool, so set the budget accordingly.

CONTENT IS ROYAL

[The agency's job is to create] content so valuable and useful that [consumers] wouldn't want to live without it.

—Jeff Hicks, chief executive officer, Crispin Porter + Bogusky[19]

Crispin Porter + Bogusky has in many ways led the way in mastering the mix of content and digital in communications. The agency's campaigns, such as those for Burger King and Domino's Pizza (in which they created a website where people order pizza and then can follow their order like a FedEx package), illustrate how it has managed to achieve crossover from advertising to content and entertainment.

Branded entertainment is on the rise, and in some cases marketers can have the last word when it comes to which shows continue and which get canned. In the case of *Chuck*, an NBC show, the support of Subway—where the lead character works—helped give the series a new lease on life.

A survey from the Association of National Advertisers found that 38 percent of members were spending more on branded entertainment in 2010 than in previous years, as an alternative to the thirty-second spot.[20]

Scott Donaton, author of *Madison and Vine*, describes how branded entertainment has become an everyday reality of the communications industry as media companies look to monetize their content.[21] To meet increased interest in branded entertainment, media agencies have created internal divisions that cater to this need. Mindshare set up Mindshare Entertainment. IPG established Ensemble, and my own agency network group, ZenithOptimedia, rolled out its global content division NewCast in multiple markets.

The CBS series *Survivor* helped create a new model for advertiser involvement in a television show thanks to Mark Burnett, who weaved in product rewards for contestants with a game of survival.

Advertising is mutating, and increased bandwidth has propelled it into all kinds of audiovisual content. Web users are taking brands into their own hands, whether it's creating Super Bowl commercials for Doritos or dropping mints into cans of soda on YouTube. One channel, the Al Gore–backed Current TV, offers viewers a forum to create shows as well as commercials.

Entertaining content is seen as more authentic. What else could explain the stampede of brands to the writers' rooms of late-night comedians? The team for Comedy Central's Stephen Colbert created an entire segment for Kraft by setting up a tongue-in-cheek fight between mayonnaise lovers and the Kraft product Miracle Whip.

PERSONALIZATION

In 2006 *Time* famously named as its person of the year You. The magazine reasoned that collaborative efforts such as Wikipedia, YouTube and MySpace defined the year much more than any single individual.

Welcome to the me generation. *Time* wrote that the web is "a tool for bringing together the small contributions of millions of people and making them matter. Silicon Valley consultants call it Web 2.0, as if it were a new version of some old software. But it's really a revolution."[22]

The individual experience is what consumers demand, what connects and engages them. Now that demand is possible to meet through technology, marketers are finding it necessary to tap into it. That started with the user experience online. The consumer's ability to interact with web content was the first step in the personalization experience. Google finds content customized to a person's search terms. Facebook pages are customized to your friend information and filtered through your news feeds.

The access to data based on behavior or stated interests is opening another door to serving up ads to users. Hulu and other video sites give you a choice of ads to view. That level of customized targeting is now offered with television ads through set-top-box data from pay-television companies or opt-in content. Mobile media provides the flexibility to build location into the messaging. The trick is in putting the bits of information back together again in a way that appeals to the viewer.

All the data is defining more customer segments that can be reached and ultimately sold to. A message that resonates with the widest group of people is relatively blunt mass media. A recession coupled with multiplying media options for targeting different segments has pushed marketers to think about whether they need to go big and reach the masses or be very selective and reach new moms or cat owners. Google's innovations and other digital advances, such as addressable advertising platforms, are helping advertisers single out the most logical target customers and the loyal enthusiasts.

Being able to pinpoint and efficiently target these micro groups with specific offers and products is making the role of Brand Media Strategy more important and effectively taking waste out of the equation. Addressable advertising trials show how much more receptive customers are when advertising messages interest them. Publicis Groupe's Starcom conducted trials in Baltimore, Maryland, and Huntsville, Alabama, in concert with sales organization Comcast Spotlight that proved that more targeted television placement increased advertising efficiency by 65 percent.[23]

The new media playbook reflects the evolving media landscape where technology has forced brands to catch up with a more wired, mobile and attention-elusive consumer. Advertising ceased to be about just the ads a fair while ago. The digital era has changed all that. The golden age of the Brand Media Strategy has arrived.

CHAPTER 3

A SHIFT FROM MEDIA PLANNING TO COMMUNICATIONS PLANNING

ENTER THE SUPER PLANNER

In today's marketing and media environment only the naïve and foolish confuse presence with impact.

—Stephen Heyer, former chief operating officer
Coca-Cola Company, now chairman and
chief executive officer, Harry & David[1]

People often ask me, "What is the difference between media planning and communications planning?" My response is that media planning is focused on reaching as many of the right audience in the right place at the right time and at the right cost as possible, whereas communications planning is less about *reaching* people than *influencing* them.

The increased scrutiny of big business by Wall Street, the growth of the internet and the intensity of the global recession that began in 2008 have resulted in a need for more rigor in sharpening the focus on the Brand Media Strategy.

ENTER THE SUPER PLANNER
AND COMMUNICATIONS PLANNING

Communications planning allows a more strategic way of determining key media choices and connection strategies. It is about moving away from the job of delivering messages to audiences and moving toward better understanding of how consumers receive and respond to communication. The starting point is the consumer, not the media channel or the discipline. When practiced at its best, communications planning not only develops the Brand Media Strategy but also informs the creative. Communications planning has already evolved to the point that important marketers are giving it high priority. Procter & Gamble and Johnson & Johnson both appointed agency of records (AORs) in the United States for communications planning.

In his book *Space Race,* Jim Taylor argues that communications planning first began with Ogilvy's formulation of a 360-degree philosophy in 1997: "Soon after came Unilever's 'fish' process which later became the 'ABC' process. Within which communications planning as a discipline was born."[2]

For a long time media strategy was based on delivering creative messages efficiently and effectively. Clients used full-service agencies that gave them a little of everything they needed, with integration between the various marketing disciplines a given.

The difficulties emerged as media agencies split off from their creative brethren as part of the great unbundling movement. This started the disintermediation between creative and media. The predominance of creative agencies as the lead agency began to be challenged as the media long tail expanded and some clients worried that creative shops defaulted to a television or print execution to address their every marketing challenge.

The advent of specialist and independent media agencies such as Carat and Zenith in Europe began by the mid-1990s. From there they moved into the rest of the world, including the United States, separating media and creative. Initially, the driving force for the separation was to consolidate the scale and volume of media buying. But new theories have arisen about how media channels influence the consumer, and rather than simply focusing on which media channels to choose, a handful of agencies saw a gap in the market and began pioneering the world of communications planning, a business essentially free from the legacy of advertising or mass media.

The focus on communications planning intensified in the 2000s, with over a dozen independent communications planning shops establishing themselves in London. The larger full-service media shops quickly caught up and the discipline gained traction globally. High-end strategy was a much better sell to clients than the fast-commoditizing buying business.

As the media marketplace evolved, summed up in the previous chapter, communications planning and the Brand Media Strategy have become more important ingredients in the advertising development process.

This was highlighted in *Advertising Age* by editor at large Matthew Creamer in April 2006 when he wrote, "As consumers' attention drifts among more and more media outlets, everyone agrees that the time is ripe for the discipline of channel planning to blossom in the US. While communications planning is more typically associated with media agencies, more full-service creative shops are incorporating into their account-planning departments the people and tools that can take apart a marketing budget in a media-agnostic way and be willing to shift spending—often away from mainline advertising."[3]

Creative agencies have experimented with communications planning as a discipline to bridge this gap. Agencies like BBH, Goodby Silverstein & Partners and JWT established internal communications planning functions. Sometimes these were called Channel Planning or Engagement Planning or Context Planning, and all had the general purpose of partnering with account planning, creative and digital to facilitate more integrated communications.

AN EVOLVING ADVERTISING
AND COMMUNICATIONS PROCESS

As the next iteration of the internet begins and online search and social media unfold, clients' need for communications planning to rationalize their relationships has become more urgent. Desire for integration and coordination has become a necessity.

This task has been made more complex by the growing number of agency relationships. For example, in addition to the creative and direct response agency partnerships, social media has brought public relations into the foreground and digital agencies have mushroomed as the demand for response- and data-driven plans has grown.

Once a brand's creative strategy was at the heart of marketing. Now clients must consider as equally important the Brand Media Strategy, and ideally the two should sit together and inform each other.

This is a departure from the mass media approach of developing creative first, with media's job being to place the ads in front of the right people. As explained earlier, context, relevance and involvement have become important components in making the communications more potent. Communications planning is about ensuring that these factors are built into the advertising process.

The Brand Media Strategy precedes the media planning process and is the principal input into the media planning brief. It also should help clients understand the best use of each touch point and how all media communication channels can be integrated.

NEW SKILLS FOR THE NEW PLANNER

Communications planning in the Google and Facebook era needs a broader set of skills and expertise beyond media planning experience and a flair for ideas.

BEING STRATEGIC

Strategy is one of the most overused and misused words in our business. People toss it around like candy on Halloween night. I've seen strategies that were really just a list of objectives. Sometimes they were tactics and initiatives. I subscribe to the Michael Porter school of strategy:

Create a unique and valuable position, involving a different set of activities. A Brand Media Strategy needs to offer unique space for the brand to occupy and own. The communications planner doesn't just plan a campaign that meets objectives but also develops a differentiated Brand Media Strategy that will deliver a competitive advantage.

Strategy requires you to make trade-offs. A Brand Media Strategy must choose what *not* to do. No client I've ever worked with has had the budget to do everything. Being strategic requires choices, such as determining where to allocate the resources that will deliver a greater return. I always worry when I read media award papers that tout "surrounding the consumer with 360° communications." It conjures throwing stuff against the wall and seeing what sticks.

Strategy involves creating fit among your activities. Brand Media Strategy works best when media ideas, initiatives and tactics combine into a bigger and more complete strategic platform or idea. This is particularly important in a world with an increasing number of touch points. The consumer consistently getting the same message is key to integrated communications.[4]

DIGITAL PROFICIENCY IS ESSENTIAL

Adding digital expertise across the agency functions has become a priority and no more so than with the communications planner. While you don't need to be fully proficient in analytic algorithms, you have to help manage digital.

In this media mash-up it doesn't make sense to have only a digital strategy or mobile strategy. Clients are looking for "a strategy." The real challenge for marketers is to integrate digital solutions into the total plan. What role do they play now, and how should the budget be allocated? Given its importance, I will deal with this specifically in chapter 10.

ACQUIRING EXPERTISE IN CONSUMER INSIGHT

Getting a feel for customers' emotional response to a category or brand I found to be the most challenging skill to develop for communications planners coming from general media agency or media planner backgrounds. Media planning has traditionally been more analytic than those other backgrounds. Evaluating the quantitative performance of media plans based on reach, frequency or cost efficiency is second nature. So is analyzing brand and purchase data or optimizing digital performance marketing campaigns. However, the notion of using intuition or gut feel makes many planners uncomfortable. My experience working with the planning teams at Optimedia was that acquiring consumer insight is a skill that can be developed. We found that once the planners had some experience in it they became more confident. I know of some media agencies that have got there by hiring creative agency account planners. Whichever way you go, insight development skills are absolutely central to establishing Brand Media Strategies in the new marketing world. We will cover insights in depth in chapter 5.

MULTICHANNEL UNDERSTANDING

Digital media adds complexity as well as opportunity to marketing plans. Traditional definitions of advertising have expanded in integrated communications. Being media neutral means deploying a wide selection: one-to-one, experiential, word-of-mouth, point-of-purchase and point-of-consumption media. The need for channel planning and selection is becoming a key requirement for brands, as is message integration across all marketing channels. The rigor and measurement that media agency planners offered in traditional media is being demanded across this vast choice of channels.

THE RISE OF THE GEEKS

Data planning has become a marketer's best friend. Performance marketing and business data to develop insights and optimize marketing communications programs are fast becoming as important as ideas and the creative process. And with that comes more rigor and confidence in the accountability and scalability of the planning.

COLLABORATION QUALITIES

If you think about the expertise we've just discussed, the communications planner really does have to be a super planner. In truth, it is rare to find all these skills in one person. That's why I've found that one of the most important qualities is the ability to collaborate and work openly and closely with those who have these skills, whether in the agency or outside it. This is not a profession for a control freak! In my experience the best magic in planning comes when it's not clear where an idea comes from, when it isn't clear where the role of one member in the client's communications team starts and another's finishes. If this can be facilitated, then you've achieved the communications planning Shangri-la.

DEVELOPING STRUCTURE
FOR COMMUNICATIONS PLANNING

The best part about being a communications planner is having the creativity and freedom to develop and present your ideas in a very individual way. I've never been an advocate of paint-by-numbers planning or insisted on following a strict process.

I've found that the best planners bring different ideas and perspectives to a problem and won't be put in a box. Two of the most impressive planners I have worked with directly are Derek Morris and Gerry Boyle out of our United Kingdom office. (Both have since moved on from planning to much bigger roles in the Publicis corporate world. Derek as chief operations officer of VivaKi UK and Gerry as chief executive officer of ZenithOptimedia UK.) Derek was a deliberator who sought input and allowed ideas to bubble and evolve for several weeks before making a decision. Gerry in contrast would lock himself in his office and emerge the next morning having nailed a strategy. Both were amazingly effective at reaching solutions, but each got there his own way.

I've worked with planners who are very visual, planners who are analytic, planners who are superorganized and planners who struggle to make it into the office before 11:00 A.M. They've all brought something special and unique to our agency's planning product. My point is that it's necessary to create a broad framework and provide the tools that help steer the planning, but it's more important to create a culture around planning and a planner community that is constantly striving to push the product forward.

At Optimedia we developed an approach to planning we call OPEN. It has a very specific philosophy and was built jointly by the agency brain trust. It is something all at the agency own. This book isn't about selling our agency ideas and philosophy, but I've provided in the following pages some helpful techniques and tools based on OPEN for planners and creative people.

A FRAMEWORK TO DEVELOP
EFFECTIVE BRAND MEDIA STRATEGIES

Perhaps it goes without saying that, while there is an element of art and intuition in communications planning, the Brand Media Strategy needs to be commercial. In other words, planners ought to be offering something that will help sell more product.

The strategy should be clearly defined and have a point of view: Who are we trying to communicate to? How should the communication work? The communications planner must also make some clear choices and tradeoffs about how and where the budget will be spent. The constant temptation for agencies and clients is to jump into specific solutions and move to the tactical too soon. They want to create a television ad or a print campaign, a website or a microsite. The focus is on executing the work or the plan. In my experience, there is often insufficient scrutiny given to budget allocation and the communications mix. This happens for obvious reasons. Specialist agencies are compensated upon execution. Even on the client side, units within the marketing department opt to protect their budgets. Separately, they have strong data about how their individual channels perform but very little on how they work in conjunction.

Within the marketer's own organizations, silos are also a struggle. A report from the Association of National Advertisers noted that "nearly 60 percent of respondents said significant change was needed in their business' approach to marketing if its function was to shift to a higher, more visionary level. One fourth of respondents said significant change was needed by their team and department."[5]

That's why the Brand Media Strategy has become a more important strategic function. Its role is to address two important questions: Where to play, and How to win. *Where* means touch points; stages of the buying process; the time of day, week and year; and individual media vehicles. *How* refers to the way media is used to drive the brand messaging harder than and differently from the competition and the way the media is leveraged to create response. Understanding where and how to advertise comes before determining what to say and the tactics that will take that message to the target consumer.

The growth of digital behemoths such as Google and Facebook have given more scope for brands to deliver more sophisticated and differentiated Brand Media Strategies. For instance, Coca-Cola and Pepsi have for over a century competed head to head. They are very similar products but use very different Brand Media Strategies. In 2010 Pepsi opted not to advertise in the Super Bowl, preferring to launch a social media campaign instead. Coca-Cola meanwhile continued to advertise in the big game.

Marketers have sought to create advertising that either reinforces brand messaging or elicits a response from the customer. These goals are not exclusive, however; marketing can do both. A mixture of media tactics and how the tactics are used is important in achieving these goals.

Two key tools that we will use are the Consumer Pathway and the Brand Media Strategy Wheel©. These are important tools to help us develop and evaluate brand media strategies and help us with decisions in communications planning.

THE CONSUMER PATHWAY

The Consumer Pathway is an important strategic platform for building the Brand Media Strategy. The Consumer Pathway, shown in figure 3.1, is an updated version of the traditional brand or purchase funnel. The funnel was based on a marketing model that put capturing consumers through brand awareness at the top of a funnel and then filtered consumers down through various stages toward purchase.

In the modern media world, that model has been turned on its head. Marketers know that the funnel model isn't always efficient, and they have developed different strategies for engaging consumers more directly at different stages at which they can influence purchase.

We know from our own purchase habits that people can buy a product without even being aware of the brand. An investor may buy a financial product solely on the basis of her financial advisor's recommendation and not need to remember the product name. Google can put a brand straight

FIGURE 3.1

Consumer Pathway						
Awareness	Involvement	Active consideration	Purchase	Consumption	Relationship/ LJ building	Advocacy
Launch a product	Increase emotional	Shift up the order of	Convert intent into action at	Improve the user	Make customer feel	Increase recommendations
Communicate a benefit	engagement before	consideration by facilitating	the point of purchase	experience	special to improve per	
Tell of an event or offer	purchase	favorable comparison			capita value	

into a consumer's active consideration, or even purchase, if he clicks a link while searching online. Brands such as Starbucks have been built through user experience and word of mouth. The coffee chain has only recently starting advertising in paid mass media.

The Consumer Pathway comprises stages of brand influence: awareness of a product or service, involvement, active consideration, purchase (conversion), consumption (usage), relationship building and advocacy.

It is important to gain insight into the consumer at each stage. Every product or service has the same basic stages, but brands within a category will have different brand hurdles. Also, the consumer relationship with a brand does not end with the purchase. It is important for planners to think beyond the purchase and consider consumption and usage. Even that isn't the end of the story, however. Advocacy begins the cycle again when the customer recommends the product or service to others.

The Consumer Pathway is the base of the marketing effort. In an ideal world, the communications planner would be able to identify strategies and tactics that would address each of the stages, but the real world has budgets. In fact, a communications plan that claims to do everything is a sure sign of insufficient clarity about what's needed or an ineffective plan.

Through media, marketers are able, but can't afford, to engage and target consumers at every stage of the purchasing process.

Awareness: The first stage is awareness, when consumers discover that a product or service may solve a problem they didn't know they had. It could be a new category, a new product, a new brand or a new or improved function or role.

This stage centers on creating visibility and recognition. Driving awareness for brands could be a significant outcome if the brand is new or there is a new benefit or idea to communicate. However, simply driving awareness is no guarantee of sales. Given that this is the most expensive to achieve in media dollars, particularly for a mass audience, setting out awareness as a communications goal is an important strategic decision.

Involvement: As consumers become more familiar with and gain more interest in the product or service, they get involved. This is the "just looking" stage, when the customer is finding out if the product or service is right and the customer is therefore open to persuasion. At this point the consumer needs experiences and information about the product. "This brand (or product) is like X, for people who need Y."

Active Consideration: Once engaged, consumers need to know more. They are doing their homework, they're perhaps asking for samples and seeking to customize. This stage is about getting the brand on the short list. Ultimately, it's about increasing brand preference and purchase intent. Active consideration means the consumer is making comparative investigations. "Why is A better than B?"

Purchase Conversion: The moment the consumer decides to buy a specific product or service but hasn't paid for it is the moment when the planner has to convert the decision to a purchase. It is the point of commitment.

Consumption (Usage): The act of consuming, or using, the product or service is the customer experience. It is the point at which consumers discover whether the product or service delivers what it promised and they're deciding whether they like it.

Relationship Building: From a business perspective, relationship building is about selling another one by encouraging repurchase or cross-selling. It is about forming a bond with consumers and reaffirming that they made the right choice. It's important to understand the promise, the contract with the customer, that was made and to deliver more than was promised.

Advocacy: Current customers speak out in support of your brand in the advocacy stage. It is the creating and enabling of word of mouth and recommendation.

In the mass media era a more conventional Brand Media Strategy would involve using media to collect consumers at the top of the funnel, to build awareness. This is still a valid strategy for a lot of brands, but in the digital era more stock is put in driving relevance and involvement, later stages in the consumer pathway. Google and ecommerce websites are driving consideration and purchase. Facebook, Twitter and other media sites give existing consumers a greater voice in the final stage of advocacy.

Media companies have become adept at leveraging their content across media platforms that affect the different stages of the Consumer Pathway. Understanding where the stages of Brand Media Strategy intersect with the Consumer Pathway is the next stage in helping the marketer reach the consumer.

THE BRAND MEDIA STRATEGY WHEEL

The wheel shown in figure 3.2 displays the chief issues a planner needs to address in the Brand Media Strategy. The first issue is understanding the

FIGURE 3.2

The Brand Media Strategy Wheel©

Note: KPI, key performance indicator.

communications challenge—establishing communication goals and defining their key performance indicators (KPIs). Then comes discovery, uncovering the target audience insight, which leads to understanding moments of receptivity. Campaign architecture is next. The Brand Media Strategy requires creating a communications platform that works in synergy with creative and involves touch-point recommendations. Finally, it is about the brand or campaign idea and its amplification, followed by integrated execution and measurement.

The rest of the book covers how we address these communications issues of the Brand Media Strategy Wheel:

Communication goals/KPIs	Chapter 4—Focusing on Outcomes, Not Outputs Chapter 12—Measurement and Metrics
Target analysis	Chapter 5—Insight over Analysis
Moments of receptivity	Chapter 8—Unlocking Moments of Receptivity
Central communication / creative platform	Chapter 7—Conducting the Orchestra
Campaign architecture	Chapter 9—Touch Point Selection
Idea amplification	Chapter 6—1 + 1 = 3 Chapter 10—Digitizing the Brand Media Strategy
Activating the plan	Chapter 11—Execution Is the X-Factor

CHAPTER 4

FOCUSING ON OUTCOMES, NOT OUTPUTS

SETTING THE BRAND MEDIA STRATEGY COMMUNICATION GOALS

A clearly articulated, inspiring and measurable communication goal is the cornerstone of a successful Brand Media Strategy. That's why this chapter may well be the most important in the book.

Having viewed many advertising campaigns, either at my own agency, Optimedia, or as a judge at award competitions, I have a few observations: All too often, the focus is on the tactics, the "how we did it" part, and planners are unable to clearly articulate the Brand Media Strategy. I have noticed that in award submissions or the trade press, the emphasis is more on how the plan was executed, particularly its creativity or innovation. Agencies lack insight into how a communications strategy directly contributed to the business outcome. And while they report impressive post-campaign metrics, they often omit a clear statement of the communication goals that should have been established at the outset.

Because advertising is multifaceted, encompassing many media, disciplines and programs, you can't lose sight of its fundamental role: to create a marketing return on investment (ROI). This chapter is about establishing such accountability at the outset.

MARKETERS UNDER GROWING PRESSURE TO SHOW RETURN ON INVESTMENT

ROI metrics have always been the sine qua non for marketers. The poor economic climate in 2008 and the subsequent recession and the growth of more accountable digital media have put executives under much greater pressure to show ROI for their programs. The need to perform is underscored by the short tenure of most chief marketing officers: on average 28.4 months, according to a January 2009 survey by recruitment specialist Spencer Stuart.[1]

Lorrie Foster of The Conference Board, marketing and management consultants, observes, "In the past, marketing awareness and brand-building activities were enough to define marketing's mission and role in a company, and to justify its budget. . . . But the focus of marketing has evolved toward more strategic, value-added activities that can be quantified and linked to corporate goals. New approaches, methodologies and tools, and technologies are making it possible to link marketing investments directly to revenues and profits, holding marketing executives accountable for achieving expected results."[2]

THE IMPORTANCE OF SETTING COMMUNICATION GOALS

In *Profitable Marketing Communications—A Guide to Marketing Return on Investment*, I explored why campaigns fail to create value for their companies.[3] There are two main reasons: First, there is not a clear understanding of the goals or the key performance indicators (KPIs) at the outset of the campaign. Second, there is no process for consistently evaluating progress, and so campaigns lack sufficient focus and consistency.

Most marketers and agencies do a very good job at validating their work, but the measurement is too often used to justify activity, rather than drive the effort. Marketing consultancy CMG Partners, Durham, North Carolina, conducted a study of four hundred top business executives. The study found that only a quarter thought their marketing was effective. All this goes to underline the importance of setting communication goals at the start of the process. And what's critical is to ensure that these goals are commercial, actionable and measurable.

OUTCOMES VERSUS OUTPUTS: WHAT'S THE DIFFERENCE?

One of the key foundations of the Brand Media Strategy is setting communication goals that are based on outcomes and not on outputs.

Reach (coverage), frequency, impressions, gross rating points (GRPs) and cost per response are everyday media metrics that are easy to measure. Because they're easy, communications planners tend to overuse them to justify recommendations. These outputs are often used rather than checkpoints on the path of campaign management, for example, "our objective is to maximize reach and frequency" or "our goal is to lower the cost per response." Over-reliance on these outputs risks chief marketing officers not approving budgets, because although measurable, these outputs don't explain how the communications strategy will help drive the marketing ROI.

Most media metrics were designed to be used as a guide for effectiveness of trading or pricing terms. They were more relevant when the goal was advertising awareness and in a world where advertising plans were driven by one or two principal media. Today, media programs typically consist of four to ten different media channels.

START WITH THE WHY

Joe Marchese, president of socialvibe, wrote in MediaPost, "It's as if the new social media reality is forcing marketers and agencies to reevaluate the reasons for advertising in the first place."[4] One of the biggest challenges to marketers is not measurement but getting chief executive officers and chief financial officers to buy into ad campaigns.

A good way to start the communications planning process is to ask a very basic question: Why advertise? Often this isn't asked. But if a company's objective is to improve profitability, then I can almost guarantee you that *cutting* advertising will improve a company's profitability within a financial year! Marketing budgets generally range from 2 percent to 20 percent of a company's expenses, which means in any year (good or bad) a chief financial officer is going to question the value of advertising. We must therefore be able to explain its value before embarking on planning.

Asking the Who, How, Where and When questions is all very well, but the most important is Why. I've found that agencies are good at recommending and developing solutions and plans but not as good at building the case for advertising itself.

Media agencies talk about engagement and awareness, and they sell eyeballs or media platforms. Creative agencies talk about how to build brands and reputation, and they sell ideas. Digital agencies focus on response and interaction. But all of us in advertising are guilty of discussing features rather than the key benefit, which is marketing ROI.

Sergio Zyman, the former Coca-Cola chief marketing officer who helped boost its worldwide annual sales volume from 9 billion to 15 billion cases, famously defined marketing success as "sell[ing] more stuff to more people more often for more money more efficiently."[5]

Let's break this down.

Selling more stuff to more people: Marketing needs to attract new customers to the brand. Advertising can help by opening new markets, promoting new products, driving in more foot traffic or increasing the rate of trial.

Selling more often: Advertising persuades people to buy more often. Reminding people when they are returning to the market to buy is as important as informing them of a new product or feature. We'll cover the theory of recency later in this chapter.

Selling for more money: Advertising has always been about selling, but there are alternatives that can help companies sell more. Price cuts and promotions can move product. For example, if Apple were to discount iPhones by 50 percent, the tech giant could sell a lot more, and probably without bothering to advertise the discount. To be able to get more for a product relies almost entirely on differentiation, and that's where branding comes in.

People will pay more for Nike iDs, Apple iMacs or BMWs, even though they might perform no better than similar products, because they are perceived as being different and better.

Selling more efficiently: Advertising offers the ability to talk to a larger audience cost effectively. If marketers could have fifteen minutes one-on-one with every potential customer, they would be very persuasive. Advertising helps companies scale a sales pitch to a broad audience.

TRANSLATING BUSINESS GOALS
INTO COMMUNICATION GOALS

Communication goals involve understanding how the communications will drive business goals. It is important not to confuse the two. "Increase sales" is not a communication goal. "Increase market share growth" is not a communication goal. They are business goals—the end game. Simply stating that we need to grow sales by X isn't particularly helpful in shaping the Brand Media Strategy. No, the role of the communications planner is to translate business goals into something that steers media, creative, PR and digital specialist teams as they perform their communications tasks.

Effective communication goals encompass two key qualities. First, they need to have a *direct line of sight* between the communications and the business outcomes. Before we can say, "Here is what we are doing" or "This is who we are targeting" or "This is where we are advertising," we need to be able to explain in simple terms how the communications is going to directly translate to the marketing or business goal. For a chief marketing officer or company board to understand how the Brand Media Strategy is going to help sell more stuff, it needs to be in well-articulated commercial terms. Second, the communication goal needs to inspire ideas and creative ways to meet the goal. In this world of ROI and accountability, we have to remember that communications is still a creative task of influencing people. The Brand Media Strategy needs a communication goal that helps the teams responsible for developing and executing the communications identify relevant, influential and penetrating platforms and activation in media.

When my media agency was planning a Denny's advertising campaign for 2009, Nelson Marchioli, the chief executive officer of Denny's, told us that getting an existing customer to make a repeat visit would increase annual sales 10 percent. And getting a lapsed customer (one who had not been to a Denny's in six months or more) to return would increase sales by 11 percent. We made our communication goal to "get people to come back to Denny's one more time." That short and simple phrase stimulated a lot of communications ideas. It made us, the media agency, think about how to get people to reappraise the brand. More importantly, it generated ideas that very directly affected guest counts, such as the free Grand Slam breakfast advertised during the Super Bowl and the innovative use of independent music artists that made late-night visits to Denny's attractive.

Developing communication goals comprises four steps:

- Break down the business goals into specifics.
- Identify how and where media can help.
- Quantify what success will look like.
- Prioritize and socialize the goals.

BREAK DOWN THE BUSINESS GOALS INTO SPECIFICS

It is important to define the business goals as specifically as possible. There's a lot packed into Sergio Zyman's "sell more stuff, to more people, more often, for more money, more efficiently." The question that you need to ask is, "Where will most of the business growth come from?"

Does a retailer want to increase foot traffic into stores, increase the average basket size or bring new customers into the franchise? Perhaps the client wants to expand distribution channels or increase frequency of purchase. Or does the company want to launch a new product or change how consumers perceive a product? Maybe the brand wants to encourage or increase trial.

Clients may not immediately tell you their goal. Maybe they're too busy or they don't know you need to know it. If so, prompt them to tell you! If you don't know where you're going, it's hard to tell someone else how to get there.

Unfortunately, none of us always has ideal, picture-perfect client briefs. A good communications planner works with what's available: Do some homework. Develop a point of view on what you think the goal should be. Talk to the other managers in the marketing or sales teams. Have a meeting with the other agency partners. Ask your chief executive officer, who might have discussed the brief with a senior member of the client. Then run your thoughts by the client before you start the planning process. Most people have an easier time telling you what they do or don't want when you present them with options.

USING THE CONSUMER PATHWAY

The Consumer Pathway provides an excellent way to frame the media communication goal (see figure 4.1). Is it a goal that requires an awareness solution? Is this a campaign that needs to change or build perceptions within a particular customer group (that is, involvement)? Does the brand have satisfactory awareness but needs to convert awareness to more sales? For Denny's, almost everyone was aware of the brand and had a pretty clear perception of it. But they had most likely visited years ago and were unaware of the significant improvements Denny's had made in their menu and restaurants in the past few years. The challenge was getting people to try the new Denny's.

FIGURE 4.1

Indirect/ Brand	Media Communication Goals					Direct/ Product
Awareness	Involvement	Active consideration	Purchase	Consumption	Relationship/ LT building	Advocacy
Role of Communications						
Launch a product / Communicate a benefit / Tell of an event or offer	Increase emotional engagement before purchase	Shift up the order of consideration by facilitating favorable comparison	Convert intent into action at the point of purchase	Improve the user experience	Make customer feel special to improve per capita value	Increase recommendations

In addition, classifying the communication goal as a stage of the Consumer Pathway pinpoints where and how the communications will drive consumers to purchase and answers the "Why advertise" question.

IDENTIFY HOW AND WHERE MEDIA CAN HELP

Brands have several marketing strategies available. In some cases they will be media led, and in other cases media is less likely to be a driver. For example, customer service or the customer experience is invariably an important factor in almost all service brands. For one of my agency's cosmetics brand clients, training make-up consultants or upgrading store beauty counters is a critical marketing priority but not likely to involve a media solution.

BUILDING AWARENESS

Launch a product, communicate a benefit or tell of an event or offer
While I advocate in chapter 2 that marketers drive involvement and relevancy, building awareness is still important for many brands. In the mass media age, driving awareness was the default and generic communication goal for advertising. The Brand Media Strategy largely concentrated on generating awareness of the creative through mass media.

If awareness is the goal, the media strategy should concentrate on effective-frequency levels. *Effective frequency* is essentially the number of times a person is exposed to an advertising message before responding. Studies have found that from one to five or more exposures are necessary, depending on factors such as the size of the print ad or the length of the commercial, the complexity of the message or the competitive clutter.

Today, planners tend to use awareness-tracking data or models to set ideal frequency levels or they use media weights to project the awareness levels generated by advertising. Once frequency levels are established, media planners and buyers seek to maximize the plan's reach, or coverage of the target audience, as efficiently as possible.

INVOLVEMENT

Increase emotional engagement before purchase

If the objective is to build the brand or drive brand reappraisal, then the communication goal will be in the involvement stage of the Consumer Pathway. Increasing brand involvement also increases awareness.

Typical goals here might include the following:

- Increase consumer understanding of the brand's strengths or its unique selling point.
- Increase the brand's appeal to target X.
- Influence consumers to see brand X as the most reliable.

McDonald's has almost ubiquitous awareness and has become a destination for family dining, a place to take your kids. When they promoted their McCafe's, the challenge was less to create awareness than to get consumers thinking of them as a destination for lattes. They developed a campaign that aimed to demonstrate that they offered lattes without the pretentiousness of a Starbucks. This included creating the website unsnobbycoffee.com.

ACTIVE CONSIDERATION

Shift up the order of consideration by facilitating favorable comparison

Conversion of brand awareness or interest into preference occurs in the active-consideration stage. This might include putting a brand in with its consideration set or providing information or opinion to help the shopper consider the brand more favorably.

Lexus in Europe discovered that their conversion of test drives to sales was significantly higher than that of Mercedes Benz, BMW or Audi. They shifted their communication goal away from a branding or awareness goal to one of getting more potential customers into show rooms for test drives. This communication goal resulted in their moving away from traditional brand advertising in business and lifestyle magazines. Instead, the Brand Media Strategy involved online advertising and partnering with five-star hotels, airports and premium vacation spots to provide test-drive information and opportunities for test drives. In addition to differentiating their media approach from competitors that outspent them, they dramatically increased the overall ROI.

PURCHASE

Convert intent into action at the point of purchase

Goals that focus on conversion of intent into action could include using media that drive pricing or trial, such as ecommerce or cost-per-acquisition media.

From awareness to reminder advertising

The emphasis on awareness-building advertising and the need to deliver effective frequency shifted in the nineties to reminder advertising, based on the concept of recency. One of the catalysts for this change was the breakthrough book *How Advertising Works,* by John Philip Jones, a professor at Syracuse University.[6]

The idea was that well-known brands of consumer packaged goods such as Coca-Cola or Tide don't need to build awareness; they already have it. The goal of the advertising should be *reminding* the consumer to buy the product at the point closest to the place of purchase. Recency theory was supported by exhaustive research and academic analysis. I recall that this book shifted the paradigm of Brand Media Strategy. Clients such as Procter & Gamble and Coca-Cola globally moved from awareness-driving to reminder-based tactics.

As a result, recency planning became a Brand Media Strategy that encouraged continuous advertising, since people are shopping every day and week of the year. Recency planning is less concerned with building brand equity than reinforcing the proposition and converting that awareness and brand knowledge to purchase.

This study still has a lot of validity for many established media brands. And despite new and emerging media, the principle of reminding consumers of your brand and placing it close to the shopping occasion, either in time or physical location, remains an effective strategy.

For example, Nestlé's Buitoni knew their customers were professional, working women wanting to pick up a meal on their way home. They targeted advertising for their chilled pasta to the end of the workday at out-of-home sites, point-of-sale locations and websites.

CONSUMPTION AND RELATIONSHIP BUILDING

The consumption and relationship-building stages often didn't involve media solutions in the past. However, media's definition is expanding, and smart agencies have used media to influence consumers even at these stages. Customer-relationship-management marketing programs that incorporate email marketing or other media partners have been known to reinforce the relationship with a brand.

Coors Light cleverly used packaging to promote the user experience. They introduced a cold-activated beer can to the market; it turned blue when it reached 44 degrees Fahrenheit.

Tony Hsieh, the chief executive officer of online shoe store Zappos.com, at the Association of National Advertisers Masters of Marketing conference in 2008 related how the company had very little media budget, so it emphasized salesperson training and customer-service interaction as the primary medium to build positive word of mouth and loyalty.

ADVOCACY

Increase recommendation

Buzz, or word-of-mouth recommendation, is increasingly important in this Facebook era. This was well demonstrated when candidate Obama shifted from the conventional political advertising strategy of targeting undecided voters to getting his advocates to persuade undecided voters.

Figure 4.2 shows a beauty care example of areas to explore for communication goals across the Consumer Pathway.

FIGURE 4.2

Beauty Care Example

	Awareness	Involvement	Active Consideration	Purchase (Conversion)	Consumption (Usage)	Relationship Building	Advocacy
Consumer Thought	I want to look good, stay looking young. I heard brand X has a new ...	I usually buy brand Y. Should I give brand X a go? Packaging looks good and it got a good review in Cosmo	I check it out. I'll ask my beautician / go to Macy's; they'll have a sampler. I wonder how much it costs?	I'll take this, please.	(Unwrap & use) Great packaging, it's so light, no greasy feeling, smells nice too.	My skin feels smoother. And their website had some great tips and advice! This is the stuff for me.	Telling friend, You should try XXX, I swear by it. Indecently, so does Sarah J Parker.
Brand Action	Launch a product Communicate a benefit Tell of an event or offer	Increase emotional engagement before purchase	Shift up the order of consideration by facilitating favorable comparison	Convert intent into action at the point of purchase	Improve the user experience	Make customer feel special to improve per capita value	Increase recommendations
	Get noticed	Engage	Close the deal	Don't let them change their mind	Deliver what you promised	Make them feel special	Help them to help you

QUANTIFY WHAT SUCCESS WILL LOOK LIKE

To define success and prioritize potential goals, you need to know where the client stands on their existing measures.

Start with overall sales and market share. The chief executive officer, chief marketing officer or head of sales will have these figures because their job depends on them. Their bonus might even be attached to the figures. They will be hugely interested if you can tell them how you're going to improve it. Then you need to drill down into the defined communication goals and establish their KPIs.

Measures for awareness, brand equity or active consideration will likely already exist, either through customer tracking or consumer attitude and usage studies. Digital data such as search inquiries, website traffic or social media tracking can provide useful measures. If those aren't available, then recommending some sort of tracking is in order. Figure 4.3 shows typical data sources for tracking campaign goals against the stages of the Consumer Pathway.

FIGURE 4.3

Measuring Campaigns against Objectives

	Awareness	Involvement	Active consideration	Purchase	Consumption	Relationship building	Advocacy
DATA SOURCES	Awareness tracking	Brand equity and image tracking	Consideration/ purchase intent tracking	Sales data	Usability tests Qualitative research	Loyalty tracking Newsletter clicks WOM tracking	PR tracking WOM tracking Buzz tracking Net Promoter

Indirect/Brand — Campaign Objectives — Direct/Product

Note: WOM, word of mouth.

HOW DO YOU QUANTIFY THE GOAL?

Now the hard part is figuring out the increase the client expects according to the KPIs. Marketers might not have defined the increase, but knowing the goal of the task is critical in deciding whether the Brand Media Strategy will work and in determining the budget.

Those benchmarks will tell you if the budget is sufficient or if the objectives are unachievable. If benchmarks don't exist, then you will have to make estimates based on past experience or other categories. In fact, for 70 percent of campaigns this is usually the case. Set a target and benchmark for future planning periods. Then ask, What revenue will this generate if this succeeds?

CASE STUDY: NEW STEEL

The American Iron and Steel Institute developed an advertising campaign to promote steel as a source of raw material. The consortium set the objective to make steel the "material of choice" for the packaging, car manufacture, construction, housing and appliance industries.

An initial investment of $20 million a year defined the terms of success and introduced surrogate measures. The consortium asked itself, "What actions or outcomes will need to occur to make it worth the investment?"

Here, they drew on the experience and expertise of teams that had implemented similar campaigns, and consulted previous case studies. They also set methods and models on which strategy and measurement would be based, and built frequent and direct interaction into the process, with people driving strategy and execution.

A research consultant made recommendations about the methodology. By meeting with key executives, the right expectations were set.

The campaign's goals were articulated in measurable terms so that everyone involved could buy into what the campaign was trying to achieve. The metrics were set based on significant improvement against the current market value and agreed with the stakeholders. They included the following:

- Awareness had to increase from 10 percent to 25 percent.
- Favorability had to move from the benchmark score of 58 to at least 70.
- To claim "material of choice," the thermometer for steel would need to move from last to first place versus its competitors.
- The positive to negative comments ratio had to move from 2:3 to 6:1.[7]

PRIORITIZE AND SOCIALIZE THE GOALS

One of the biggest factors in campaign failures is insufficient budget to deliver the goals. Trying to do too much with too little budget is a recipe for disaster. It comes from an unwillingness to make hard choices in setting the communication goals.

A SINGLE GOAL IS BEST

Having too many objectives ensures a lack of clarity. I really do subscribe to Napoleon's axiom that "one bad general is worth two good ones," or one goal is always better than two. Having too many goals creates a lack of accountability and clarity. I always worry when a marketer says, "Our goal is to drive sales, create buzz, drive awareness, build consideration and grow the brand." I try to discourage clients from tracking and targeting a dozen metrics. Juggling so many metrics dilutes goals. Several goals will be partially achieved, but the most important one will not be fully achieved.

Select a primary goal, one that can be consistently tracked across all efforts. With that one goal in mind you can create measurable objectives and keep all tactics focused on them. When you achieve those objectives, you're in a good position to prove your worth and defend your budget.

PRIORITIZING GOALS

When you can't have just one primary goal, which is often the case, list the goals. By each one note what metric you would use to judge it. How would improving those metrics change things? Rank the goals in terms of what's important and which would make the biggest difference in terms of sales. Which would be most likely to drive the primary business goal? There is no need for absolute accuracy as this exercise is only to indicate a direction. Then suppose you invested 90 percent, 75 percent or 50 percent of the budget—how does that affect the goal? Move to the second goal in your ranking. This time, suppose you spent 50 percent, 33 percent or 15 percent of the budget. What effect would that have on the goal?

Repeat for each potential goal.

BRANDING THE GOAL

When I was a planner working on Procter & Gamble campaigns, I recall, the company was great at marketing their marketing: coming up with a catchy phrase to describe a goal. For example, Procter & Gamble talked about "winning at the two moments of truth." Those two moments are when the consumer is about to buy and use the product.

There's merit in branding a communication goal. It makes it more memorable and inspirational. It helps everyone from the chief executive officer to the frontline sales and customer-service teams grasp the concept. Be sure to market the goal inside and outside the company.

The goal should ideally describe an action that involves the consumer. Wal-Mart's chief marketing officer, Stephen Quinn, says that his company's goal is to help deliver true value to customers.[8] The company's winning marketing campaign in 2009 was "Give people ideas to save money." At Coca-Cola the goal for one brand team was to convince young men that Coke Zero tastes like regular Coke. Similarly, at computer giant HP, the goal was to make personal computers cool again. A single rallying cry will inspire solutions, and there's no need to keep it secret. If everyone knows what your strategy is, then they can help you execute it.

QUESTIONS IN SETTING THE COMMUNICATION GOALS

1. Does the communication goal have a clear line of sight to the business goal?
2. What stages of the Consumer Pathway does the goal target?
3. What is the primary goal?
4. Does the goal inspire the communications?

CHAPTER 5

INSIGHT OVER ANALYSIS

FINDING A WAY IN FOR
THE BRAND MEDIA STRATEGY

*Data is not information, information is not knowledge, knowledge is
not understanding, understanding is not wisdom.*

—Cliff Stoll and Gary Schubert[1]

THE ROLE OF CONSUMER INSIGHT IN
DEVELOPING THE BRAND MEDIA STRATEGY

In the media world we are awash with statistics. We love the sanctuary of
data. It's safe. It's predictable. But does it tell us anything new? Demographics, psychographics, audience figures distract from the importance
of personalizing marketing. Communication should be about focusing on
people rather than consumers. *People* are individuals, new moms, an office
worker on her lunch hour or a young family buying their first new car.
They're not a number on a spreadsheet.

As a communications planner, it's crucial to be consumer facing rather
than media facing. Remember, media planning is about reaching the right
people at the right places; communications planning is about influencing

people. And an important part of influencing is to understand how the group you are trying to connect with thinks, behaves and lives their lives. And yes, of course, how they consume media and respond to communications.

Analyzing audience surveys or syndicated media or product reports alone won't give you those answers. Yes, they can tell you how many people are watching this or reading that. But clues to how they might respond better to different communication strategies? Much less likely. Media surveys commoditize consumers into common audience demographic groups. So a ratings point on the History Channel or ESPN is treated exactly the same despite being very different programming attracting viewers with different mind-sets.

Using the same syndicated data that all your competitors have will lead to the same strategies and solutions, hardly the formula for creating distinct and penetrating campaigns. Using the same research that others use encourages premium pricing, as advertisers in a category chase the same positions and the same titles or television shows. The old way of doing things assumes that media works the same way for every brand. This dictates that advertisers compete on share of voice by outspending competitors.

For a communications planner, having insight about your target is what differentiates your plan. To have insight, the communications planner needs to be the consumer's best friend.

FROM WHERE TO HOW

Developing insights is the key to unlocking a way in for the Brand Media Strategy, insights into not just which media or marketing communication touch points to advertise in, but also how to use those media.

Syndicated media audience surveys from the likes of Nielsen, Arbitron, TNS and comScore provide extensive data on which media audiences spend time where. They do exactly what they are designed to do, which is to establish the scale of target audiences. Mass media strategies to maximize reach and frequency use this audience data to establish awareness. In the shift from the mass media era to today's of targeting your audience, consumer insight is the key to connecting to your audience by using a broader selection of touch points to communicate.

Digital data from performance marketing campaigns has added more dimension to traditional media research. For example, Google's tools and web tracking have allowed richer insight into the consumer's decision-making process and better understanding of consumers' reactions to ad messaging and their post-campaign buying habits. Thanks to social listening, we can get consumers' immediate feedback to develop the all-important insight.

As shown in figure 5.1, insight has facilitated the shift from media planning to communications planning.

ACCOUNT PLANNING ESTABLISHED INSIGHT IN ADVERTISING

Agency account planning is very much the forebear to communications planning.

FIGURE 5.1

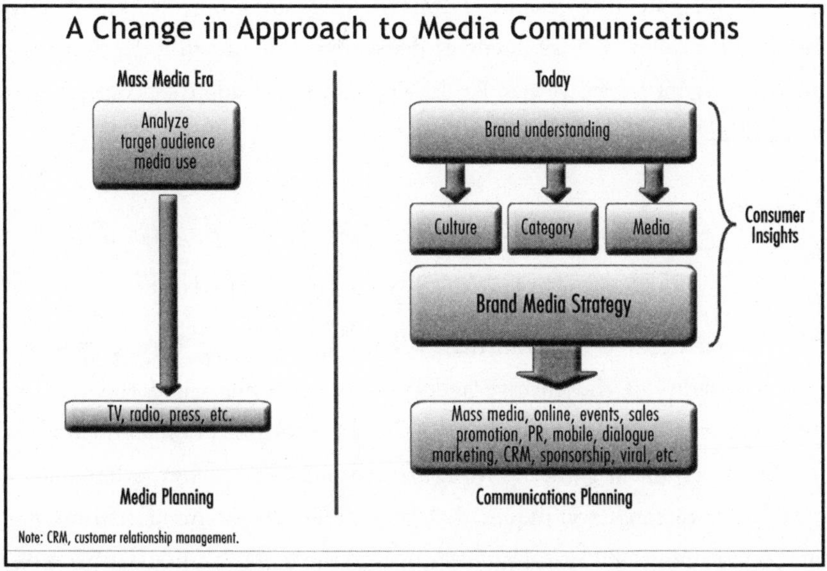

A Change in Approach to Media Communications

Mass Media Era

Analyze target audience media use

TV, radio, press, etc.

Media Planning

Today

Brand understanding

Culture   Category   Media

Brand Media Strategy

Consumer Insights

Mass media, online, events, sales promotion, PR, mobile, dialogue marketing, CRM, sponsorship, viral, etc.

Communications Planning

Note: CRM, customer relationship management.

Account planning was invented in the United Kingdom by Stanley Pollitt in 1965. He was a founding partner of Boase Massimi Pollitt (BMP, now BMP DDB) and established account planning by bringing in a researcher to work as an equal partner with the account manager in briefing the creative departments. In 1968 the London office of J. Walter Thompson established an account planning department. Account planning was exported to the United States in 1982, when Jay Chiat set up an account planning team. Chiat Day went on to become one of the most successful agencies in the eighties, growing its billings from fifty million dollars to seven hundred million dollars in ten years. Many US creative shops followed suit.

In the nineties, account planning grew exponentially and today has become a mainstay function in creative agencies. Chris Cowpe, owner of the Caffeine Partnership, a management consultancy, and former chief executive officer of BMP DDB in London, observes, "To be truly effective, advertising must be both distinctive and relevant, and planning helps on both counts."[2]   ⟋ Pete Campbell

The primary responsibility of account planners is to understand the target audience and to be its ambassador throughout the ad development process. Insights have become an important element in developing creative work. They help creative agencies decide what to say in advertising and help the agency creative people develop ideas and ads that connect with their targets.

CONSUMER INSIGHT: THE ACCOUNT PLANNER VERSUS THE COMMUNICATIONS PLANNER

We've often debated at Optimedia, "What is the difference between the consumer insights of the creative agency account planners and those of the media agency communications planner?" Often the line between them blurs.

Both approach gathering insight in similar ways. They're looking for qualitative research techniques that provide an unstructured environment and opportunities for revealing insights into the more emotional aspects of a brand. They both use traditional one-on-one approaches such as interviews and focus groups as well as more creative approaches such as accompanied shopping, word associations, use of visual prompts, video montages, projective techniques and consumer diaries. Both types of planners may also seek quantitative, behavioral and attitudinal data from long-term studies to uncover social and cultural changes. They use primary and secondary research sources such as published market reports, usage and attitude surveys and awareness-tracking studies.

Derek Morris, chief operating officer for VivaKi UK, who has run both communications planning and account planning departments, said to me once that creative agencies are generally much better at developing insights than their media agency planning counterparts: "They've been doing it longer, have more resources and [have] built more time into their planning process." Media agency planners would do well to learn from them.

The difference between the two, however, is that account planning is looking at insight to help the creative teams determine what to say. They want to understand what's going on in consumers' lives so they can say, "This is what the brand stands for" or "This is why it's different" and "This is why consumers should choose it." A communications planner is focused on insight that can help determine how and where to say those things. The key question to keep asking when developing the Brand Media Strategy is, How are people going to be more engaged with the communications?

In illustration of the difference between account planning insight and communications planning insight, Chris Pyne, my agency's former New York head of planning, cites interviews he and the creative agency's account planning director for L'Oréal conducted with beauty editors from Hearst Magazines. The purpose was to better understand how they could develop communications for Garnier beauty products. The creative agency account planner asked the editors, "What do you see as the difference between French and American women when it comes to beauty products?" while Chris asked, "What are you doing to get people to read or engage with your editorial?" Contrast these questions with what a traditional media planner might have asked: "Who reads the magazine?" The communications planner's and the account planning director's questions created valuable insight into how to communicate.

Account planning and communications planning roles can and should be a team effort, often with much crossover. The client might ask whether they are paying twice for both, but if you don't have crossover, you don't get integration. The enemy of integration is silos in which people keep to their own spaces.

Sometimes an account planner's consumer work can set the agenda for the media strategy. For example, the global campaign conducted by the bank HSBC uncovered the importance that international business people place on local market knowledge. The campaign developed by Lowe & Partners Worldwide promoted HSBC as "the world's local bank," by depicting the differences in countries' interpretations of certain topics. The original launch ad, "Football," displayed versions of footballs from the United States, England and Australia. Our agency planned this campaign with HSBC and Lowe, and we translated the creative campaign into the now famous international airport program. We reinforced the idea of local knowledge by placing ads inside flight boarding walkways, where international passengers would view them. This component of the media campaign proved hugely successful.

Insights into media use can be very important and influential in the creative strategy. For example, the planning agency that developed Unilever's campaign for Dove discovered that 80 percent of women feel worse about themselves after reading a women's magazine. From that they developed the "Campaign for Real Beauty" and advertising that depicted real women of all sizes, shapes and colors.

That's where communications is becoming more interesting and the reason why there's a need for more collaboration among the planning teams at the different agency disciplines. Where I've found communications planning to really work well is when it informs or adds to the creative insight process.

Media, digital and creative agencies tend to want to maintain their separation. Sometimes battles over turf, fees and egos get in the way of collaboration. But I've always found that most communications planners and account planners care less about politics and more about the work. They want to be collaborative and are more open to working in tandem. We had a consumer-packaged-goods client with an interesting process for facilitating collaboration. The brand chairs a meeting at which creative, media and digital planners co-develop a campaign strategy. Their only rule is that no one in account management is allowed to participate!

Memo to chief marketing officers and agency account management: Put all the planners together in one room and you will get a better and more insightful product.

A MORE COMPLEX AND VARIED CONSUMER

Peter Francese, a demographics trends analyst, has projected what the 2010 census will tell us about US consumers. "The concept of an 'average American' is gone, probably forever," he writes. "The average American has been replaced by a complex, multidimensional society that defies simplistic labeling."[3]

The message to marketers is clear: No single demographic, or even handful of demographics, neatly defines the nation. There is no such thing as "the average American consumer." Francese highlights that the 2010 census will show that the classic American family—married couple[s] with children—will account for only 22 percent of households.

Francese projects that the most widespread type of US household is a married couple without children, followed closely by single-person households. The 2010 census gave Americans fourteen choices to define household relationships. Mr. Francese says this will "enable the Census Bureau to count, not only traditional families, but also the number and growth of blended families, single-parent families and multigenerational families, as well as multiple families doubling up in one household."[4] That presents boundless opportunities for marketers and media to develop strategies for how they target and segment households.

MICROTRENDING

Mark Penn is the chief executive officer of the global communications firm Burson-Marsteller and president of Penn, Schoen and Berland, a market research firm. He has advised both former president Bill Clinton and Secretary of State Hillary Rodham Clinton in her presidential run, as well as former British prime minister Tony Blair and former Microsoft chief executive officer Bill Gates. As President Clinton's pollster in his 1996 reelection campaign, Penn identified the microtrend of soccer moms and their importance to the campaign.

Penn argues that small groups of people who share an intense choice or preference that is often counterintuitive have been undercounted or missed by companies, marketers, policymakers and others. A microtrend can be created by as few as three million people, or about 1 percent of the US population. Even if that group doesn't grow, it can still have enormous impact on society.[5]

The importance of connecting with these groups is huge. One group identified by Penn is moms over forty-five who play computer games. They are the fastest-growing group of gamers but hardly a group normally targeted by gaming companies. Nintendo targeted this group in its launch of the interactive Wii. They set up Wii parties for the "alpha moms," a target segment of socially connected households in several major markets, and ran print advertorials illustrating how playing Wii could improve a mom's family time.[6]

The internet, more dynamic customer data and tightly targeted long-tail media have helped to make it more feasible and economical to identify and market to these microtargets. Microtargeting through digital advertising networks gives brands the ability to focus on their markets with specific messaging, helping marketers mine user data to find the specific content viewed and create behavioral profiles. Newer ways of communicating, such as addressable television and internet radio, open microtargeting across all media. And we're starting to see personally addressed billboards that respond to mobile phone signals. Remember the scene from the film *Minority*

Report, in which Tom Cruise is greeted with personally targeted ads? That doesn't seem so futuristic anymore.

Penn explains that people should care about microtrends "because they are the new driving force behind our society and our future. Our society is blessed with unprecedented choices and people are expressing those choices in ways that create new markets, new affinity groups, and new movements. And if you are relying on conventional wisdom to find them, you will be left behind because CW [conventional wisdom] is a lagging indicator not a leading one."[7]

COMING UP WITH INSIGHTS

Developing insights can be a challenge for planners. There are as many techniques to develop insights as there are planners. Let me try to open this black box a little.

WHAT ARE YOU LOOKING FOR?

Look for clues about when, where and how consumers can be influenced, and have relevant, motivating, valuable brand experience. We are trying to build strategic platforms or big ideas to communicate based on consumer insight.

THE INSIGHT DEVELOPMENT PROCESS

Consumer insights can come to you while in a supermarket aisle, as part of a chance conversation with a customer service manager, or from a newspaper article. Agencies use many techniques to gather observations. Techniques come in and out of vogue. For example, I am definitely seeing a movement away from the traditional focus group. Observation techniques such as ethnographic studies and online monitoring have become the order of the day. Since insights can come from anywhere, you need to start by casting the net wide. The skill is to ask probing and thoughtful questions. There are a ton of sources and techniques to trawl.

The Brand Media Strategy Insight Development Process (figure 5.2) is a six-stage process that my agency uses to develop hypotheses to test, quantify and validate. The hypotheses are developed out of points of view that come from conversations, observations and discovery. Coming up with a hypothesis and then testing it is a proven approach. It's very difficult to directly ask consumers what they want; they aren't marketing experts. As legendary marketer and Apple chief executive officer Steve Jobs once said, "A lot of times, people don't know what they want until you show it to them."[8]

FIGURE 5.2

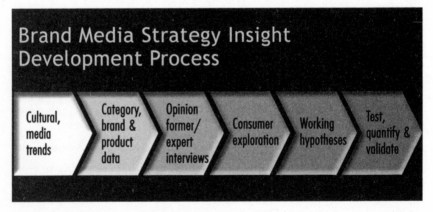

QUESTIONS THAT CAN UNCOVER BRAND MEDIA INSIGHTS

The insight process has five important questions to ask.

What types of contexts make the messaging more relevant to consumers?

At Optimedia, we refer to this as the *receptivity insight:* the context or media environments that help the communications be more influential or effective in conveying the brand message.

*Which media experiences influence branding and which drive
behavior?*

Different combinations of touch points or media impact consumers differently. Newspaper and radio can be strong at driving response. Search can drive traffic. Video helps to influence the brand. They all bring value and options for a planner. Gaining insight into their impact in relation to the communication goals is important for a planner to determine.

*What marketing efforts are our customers noticing? Do they
attribute them to the correct brands?*

Insight into the brand category and how the brands use communications tells you how the Brand Media Strategy can differentiate the brand.

*What motivates people to be brand evangelists or share virally
with other consumers?*

Creating brand conversations, discussed in chapter 6, relies on finding cultural factors, elements in the brand category and characteristics of the brand sharers that give the communications more legs.

*What's the propensity that propels my customers toward my brand
or category?*

Most insights center on the consumer, but we need to know how the insights relate to the specific brand category and customers we target.

APPROACHES ON GATHERING INSIGHT

Of the techniques listed here, many I learned from creative shops, some from clients and design agencies and some we at Optimedia developed ourselves.

Some simple things can be done from your desk. Better still is getting out and talking to people. Being interested in people is a prerequisite to being a communications planner. There are quantitative ways of gathering insights from surveys, trackers, household panels and product tests.

Qualitative methods might involve examining perceptions or emotions, doing ethnographic research or simply observing what people do.

CAST THE NET WIDE

Insights don't have to be centered only on the consumer. They can be about products, or the cultural environment or the market in general (figure 5.3). It's important to keep in mind not only the Consumer Pathway but also current media trends. Are customers now paying for media by subscription? If so, how does that affect the acceptance of advertising? Look at consump-

FIGURE 5.3

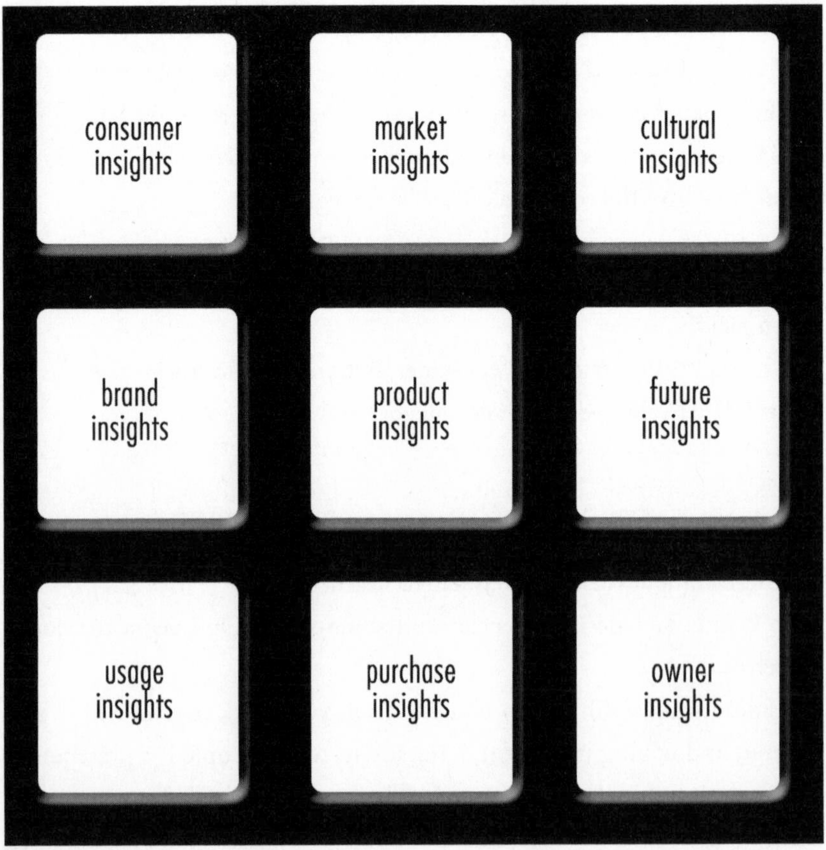

consumer insights	market insights	cultural insights
brand insights	product insights	future insights
usage insights	purchase insights	owner insights

tion rituals and the motivations behind them. What is the attachment consumers have to certain products?

Russell Evans and Kamal Tahir suggest that the best insights arise from a healthy information ecosystem with technology that facilitates a high level of interoperability. A lot of published data, such as syndicated market audits, customer and retail data and trends reports, gives enormous insight.

Cultural trends can create brand communication opportunities for brands. The famous YouTube video of the Filipino prisoners who re-created Michael Jackson's "Thriller" music video sparked imitations. T-Mobile's agency leaped in by filming a group dance video at London's Liverpool Station that became an online advertising sensation.

TALK TO EXPERTS

Before you talk to consumers, speak to people who know the business. For example, tap the people who work for a trade body or association, editors of trade or consumer publications, frontline salespeople and account managers, suppliers to the brand, bloggers on the subject or retailers. British ad agency HHCL, working for the UK Automobile Association, spoke to association phone operators and found that members talked about how friendly the AA repairmen were.

Tap into the collective knowledge inside the client's company. Draw on the experience and judgment of people in the business by interviewing the client company's sales force, service departments and retailers who deal with the end customers. Retailers think about the business all day. They see what customers are actually doing, rather than what they say. They observe why people don't buy the product. They can also steer you in a direction to probe further.

LOOK AT WHAT PEOPLE DO, NOT WHAT THEY SAY

Observation is a powerful technique for developing consumer understanding. Here are a handful of helpful approaches.

Michael Harvey, global consumer planning director at beverage giant Diageo, offers this advice: "Observing consumer behaviour in the on and off-trade: getting out and watching people in-situ is free and a great source of insight."[9]

HIT THE STREETS

Nike used street teams to listen to urban tastemakers under the guidance of urban marketer Come Chantrel. Chantrel took the techniques he had used for marketing and pre-testing music at Loud Records and put them to work for the sneaker company on the street, with resounding success.

Nike is still using this process. Having failed in the skateboard sneaker market with a flashy ad campaign, Nike succeeded by listening to a panel of respected skaters. Now, it sells the shoe line only in independent skate shops, advertises only in skateboard magazines and offers sponsorships to carefully chosen skaters. By listening before it speaks, it has achieved the delicate art of being cool without trying too hard.

JOURNALING

Tom Neveril, president of Storybrand Consulting, a market intelligence firm in Santa Monica, California, advocates journaling.

He asks interviewees to fill in calendar pages for every half hour of their activities and their train of thought during those times. He explains that the entries should be made near the time of the experience and aimed at capturing the memories of the customer experience, like car shopping. He dubs this approach "Outlook calendar journaling." Neveril also suggests conducting ethnographic research, in which people are observed in their natural environment going about their everyday activities, whether brushing their teeth or cleaning their kitchen or visiting a car dealership.

"Whether you gather recalled stories, journals or observations of the 'here and now,' you will encounter apparent hypocrisy. That's OK," writes Neveril. "Contradictions can be very revealing. But don't bother pointing it out to the interviewee. That will only cause them to withdraw. And giving someone a reality check would upset the natural order and meaning that they've created in their lives. And if you want to get to know the real person, you must make them comfortable in their sometimes irrational skin. So if you want to know how your customers will behave in the future, don't ask for more of their opinions. Just take a look at their behavior."[10]

DIGITAL INSIGHTS CAN BE POWERFUL

Using Search to Develop Planning Strategy

My experience is that search data provides an insightful source of consumer behavior for planners.

Keyword data results open up unexpected avenues of thinking because the results are based on actual consumer behavior rather than our assumptions. For example, surveying search patterns on Google tells us when in the holiday retail season consumers start researching items such as perfume. This gives us insight into the right time to plan the scheduling of the advertising. When customers research products, they are more receptive to the communications.

Keyword data suffers none of the downsides of conventional research such as research effect, because all of the behavior is natural and results can be manipulated and furthered to meet your needs. The results can be constantly updated, without continually commissioning new rounds of research.

Keywords as the Stimulus for the Planning Strategy

When used appropriately, search tools are a strategic weapon for brands and marketers. Because search is at the bottom of the buying funnel, it provides valuable insight into the effectiveness of other brand-building channels. You can better understand the efficiencies of TV, print, sponsorships and other activities by analyzing how changes in spending in those channels are reflected in search behaviors.

Our search team at Optimedia analyzed a paid-search campaign of one of our luxury clients and came across an interesting insight. Although we used different combinations of branded search phrases, such as "engagement rings," "watches" and "jewelry," we found that once people clicked through to the brand's website, they would check out nearly all the product lines. This led us to consider whether the client should continue to support product advertising or focus on promoting the brand or the product range.

Listening Online

One of the best types of consumer research that you can do at your desk is tracking conversations online to understand what people are saying and thinking about a brand or category.

Jason Kilar, the chief executive officer of Hulu, says that he sometimes checks Twitter twenty times a day. There are twenty-four hundred Hulu-related tweets a day. "It's a transparent engine," he observes. "I've always said that our brand is what people say about us when we're not in the room and this is the best tool for hearing what people are saying."[11]

Beauty giant L'Oréal conducted research that involved listening to what women were saying to each other about hair coloring. It found that women don't talk about vitamin B_{12} strengtheners with their friends. They'd rather talk about "What my hair will look like in that color." That insight led L'Oréal to create the swatch flip pad, in which women pull a small tuft of hair through the pad to see what their hair color looks like in different L'Oréal shades. Over 85 percent of the women who received the swatch flip pad talked about it with five or more friends.[12]

BMW's Mini division hired listening vendor MotiveQuest to mine online conversation data and found that Mini owners "view their cars as a blank canvas onto which they could project their personality."[13] The firm then worked with the agency Butler, Stern, Shine & Partners, Sausalito, California, to develop a campaign that included personalized messages to drivers via digital billboards based on digital identification chips in their cars. MotiveQuest then used its Online Promoter Score methodology to track how many people recommended the brand to others online. They found that the score could predict sales impact one month out.

MEDIA CONSUMER INSIGHTS

I believe that insights derived from how consumers are using media can drive incredibly influential communications. We've talked to editors of women's magazines to understand how they address women about today's fashion and beauty. We scour the *Wall Street Journal* or the *Financial Times* to better understand what's keeping chief executive officers up at night. Similarly, Wired.com has rich insight into whether new products have support from tech opinion leaders.

How the Millennial generation interacts with social media provides a source for ideas of how brands can interact with them. For example, they spend a lot of time on sites such as Facebook, which have become important social currency for young women. To take advantage of that insight, cosmetics giant Estee Lauder photographed in-store makeovers that young women could post to their profile pages on social network sites.

Social media insights reveal how consumers interact with brands, other consumers and social media. Burger King conducted a campaign based on a social insight: as a collection of digital friendships grew, each friend was less valuable. Their tagline was "Friendship is strong but the Whopper is stronger," and the campaign rewarded customers for axing friends from social networks.

MTV revamps its schedule from top to bottom every few years, as the MTV generation is constantly evolving. The MTV generation, once Generation X, has shifted to Generation Y. At a program presentation MTV made to advertisers and agencies, the company told advertisers, "MTV doesn't try to reflect the latest trends; they are trying to anticipate them."[14] Therefore its programs—irreverent reality dramas, documentaries covering social issues such as cyber bullying, twenty-something directors reporting on authentic stories—capture a consumer hugely interesting to advertisers.

WHICH TARGET DO WE FOCUS ON?

The question for many planners is which type of user to focus on: a current user or a heavy user, a potential user or an influential user, a purchaser or a gatekeeper. There's no single answer here, because every category, brand and campaign requires something different.

Often the brand manager will take the lead and have ideas on whom to target. Brand managers likely have their own data and insights to share. That's a good place to start. But it never hurts to challenge the target.

Mass media thinking leans toward *maximizing audience reach* in the hopes of generating more sales. But specific brands aren't and never will be bought by everyone, far from it, so this strategy leads to inefficient spending.

Consumer-packaged-goods marketing tends to target the household shopper. This group is broad, usually too broad, making it more difficult to gain a penetrating or discerning insight.

An adage in our business says that 80 percent of a brand is bought by 20 percent of the public, but a study released in 2008 documented that a much smaller number accounted for the vast majority of sales for the average packaged-goods brand.[15] A survey of 1,364 consumer-packaged-goods brands in 23,000 stores and 54 million homes found that only 2.5 percent, or one in forty people, account for 80 percent of the average brand's sales. These are the loyal customers who return time and again to buy the products they favor—the core customers. Using existing proprietary research and a little arithmetic, it is easy to identify the size or character of the core group for any brand. Repeat purchase from existing high-volume customers is an important strategy.

Trying to target everyone is unlikely to bring success. Chase one primary audience and maybe a secondary audience. Ask, What is the 20 percent, or 10 percent, that represents the biggest chunk of profitable business? Then ask, Which part of the consumer pathway are we trying to shift? Is this campaign about awareness or getting on the shopping list? Some brands have had success focusing on the 20 percent of the customer base that represents the heaviest user. For Denny's we focused on the breakfast superfan; for sports drink Lucozade Sport they targeted the serious athlete.

Decide whether the campaign is intended to support the brand or reposition the brand. Are there factors inhibiting the brand's growth? Quantify the group of users that has the greatest impact on sales. Ask yourself which target will be more influenced by advertising/communications. When I worked on the Coca-Cola account, most of the drink was sold to household shoppers who purchased it in two-liter bottles at supermarkets. But Coke focused their media on teens because they figured they couldn't afford to target everyone. They knew that being relevant to teens was more important in establishing long-term brand loyalty and value.

GATHERING AND FILTERING INSIGHTS

It's relatively easy to have many insights. It's much harder to have one or two really powerful ones.

So you collect and collate a stack of cultural trends, media trends, category trends, attitudes, usage and communications receptivity insights. The next step is to filter and screen them. Stick them on a wall—literally. And then subject them to the following questions, tossing aside the ones that fail to meet the test. It's a brutal but telling process.

Is the insight fresh or bold or new?

Is the insight something that makes everybody think differently about the brand or how to communicate? If it does, then it will help differentiate the brand strategy and be more competitive.

Dove's "Campaign for Real Beauty" uncovered the insight that women were tired of fake images of beauty. They wanted to take good care of the body they had, make the most of the "real me." This went well beyond women's views of functional product use and into emotional territory. Amplifying this perspective of beauty hadn't ever been articulated in the category.

Is the insight a discovery about your consumer that opens the door for your brand?

Many so-called insights in marketing are really observations. They don't open the door to an opportunity, because they don't go deep enough. To get a true nugget of insight, you need to dig deeper and keep asking Why, like an inquisitive toddler, till you hit gold. While working on a campaign for a bath oil product for Unilever, Mindshare planners found that American women preferred a quick morning shower and European women preferred to unwind with a bath at night. If Unilever could persuade more American women to take some time for themselves at the end of the day, they could sell more Dove Cream Oil.

Can it travel?

A truly good insight has the ability to be executed in many different media. If you find it difficult to translate the idea into an immediate media campaign, then it probably isn't going to fly. A great insight should allow multiple executions, or at least a starting point for the communications plan. Take Folgers Coffee, for example. We used to all think that the ability to brew a good cup of coffee for our annoyingly picky friends was an effective measure of our self-worth. But then the people at Folgers uncovered a simple, obvious, but nevertheless earth-shattering, insight: coffee is mostly about waking up, and we wake up to the smell of the coffee before we take a sip. This insight drove dozens of different activation ideas and helped take the business from a 17 percent market share to 36 percent. Their current tag: "Coffee that matches your morning mood."

Does the insight influence product use or purchase?

The insight must have relevance to what's happening in people's lives and it must connect to a product. The insight with our client T-Mobile was that 68 percent of all mobile phone calls were made to five people, so they developed a product that gave unlimited calls to five people, which we helped to promote with the line "Who's in your fave five?"

Does the insight tell how to make the messaging more engaging?

Message placement can make the messaging more engaging. For example, television coverage of cycling often includes aerial shots. Nike thought these were a media opportunity and chalked the roads with messages of support. The messages got the attention of riders, including Lance Armstrong, and of television viewers when the messages were caught on camera by helicopters.

TESTING THE INSIGHT

Once you have three to four insights that can be translated into a hypothesis about ways to communicate, test them. This is where quantitative research comes in. Which insight has the most resonance? What is the scale of the insight; how many consumers respond to it? Test it across different markets, so you have more than a Northeast or West Coast perspective, and then ask, How differentiating is it?

QUESTIONS TO ASK IN THE INSIGHT GATHERING STAGE

1. What places can you look for insights?
2. How can insights help you decide how to communicate to consumers?
3. What questions need to be asked?
4. Whom do we target?
5. Can this insight help us influence the consumer to purchase?

CHAPTER 6

1 + 1 = 3

SPARKING CONSUMER BRAND CONVERSATIONS THROUGH MEDIA

THE POWER OF FREE

Ironically, as a media agency whose business model largely depends on buying media, my agency has invested millions of dollars in trying to understand and measure the value of nonpaid media. We understand that advertising is just one contributor to building brands. There are plenty of others. Today, the relevance and importance of word of mouth has a greater than ever proportion of the mix.

Brand Media Strategy in the mass media age used to be about managing your paid media communications. Thanks to Facebook, Google and any number of other digital methods of sharing information, earned media (also referred to as free media) and content creation have become integral parts of the communications mix and strategy.

Prompting and influencing consumer conversations can build new brands and promote existing ones. Everyone in the marketing business, whether in politics or packaged goods, is taking note. Thinking outside the box of traditional mass media is a given in this business, and one of the areas where that thinking is useful is in generating consumer conversations to amplify the brand. But the choice is not between paid or earned media. Advertising and word of mouth can drive each other and enhance the overall effect. This chapter is dedicated to promoting such a view; hence the title, 1 + 1 = 3.

The ZenithOptimedia Touchpoints ROI Tracker is a database our agency network built from consumer interviews to evaluate the influence different marketing communication channels have on brand purchase. Its data covers 145 categories in 37 countries. One of the most revealing findings of this research was that purchase is influenced most strongly by friends and family, followed by aftersales service, colleague recommendations and specialist recommendations.

For those wondering how much traditional media influences purchasing, figure 6.1 shows that television advertising ranked sixteenth and print advertising twentieth.

When the ad world was driven by the mass media, word-of-mouth or marketing PR was a separate line item on the marketing plan. However, word of mouth has such great influence in brand decision making that we have to consider how media can drive it.

WORD OF MOUTH DRIVES SALES

Tremor, a word-of-mouth organization formed by Procter & Gamble, found three reasons why consumer advocacy is important to driving sales.[1]

1. Word of mouth instills confidence: Many recommendations come from people you know, which reduces the emotional risk of following a recommendation.
2. A personal stake: Nothing creates loyalty like advocacy. It's a lesson straight from cognitive psychology. It means that the simple act of recommending a product gives the recommender a personal stake in its success and more reason to remain a loyal user—and continued advocate.

FIGURE 6.1

Top-Twenty Most Influential Marketing Contacts on Purchase

1. Friends & family recommendations
2. Aftersales service
3. Colleague recommendation
4. Specialist recommendation
5. Personal use of brand
6. Brand received as a gift from a friend
7. In-store product tester/sampler
8. Comparison websites
9. Seeing others with brand
10. Expert recommendations
11. Independent reviews
12. Free gift with purchase
13. Packaging
14. Sales brochures/retailer catalogues
15. Salesperson recommendation
16. TV advertising
17. Internet search
18. Loyalty schemes
19. Brand websites
20. Print articles

Source: ZenithOptimedia Global database, August 2010.

3. Increased perceived value: It's a simple equation. A person who advocates on behalf of a product becomes more appreciative of the product. This strengthening of perceived value translates into increased trial and loyalty.

Similarly, word of mouth drives awareness. A survey from Kantar Media, formerly TNS Media Intelligence, showed that an advertising campaign's awareness among those who had generated or received brand word of mouth was 200 percent higher than among those who had not generated any word of mouth. As more and more brands crowd into the marketplace, consumers must navigate myriad choices and advertising message clutter. They turn to the internet for advice and insight.

WORD OF MOUSE

To understand the increasing importance of word of mouth in the media mix, you have to understand the effect the internet is having on personal recommendation. Mainstream adoption of the internet has increasingly enabled word of mouth's role in brand decisions.

Thanks to Google and myriad other online venues, "word of mouse" has real scale. With search, consumers can find content and information more easily and more efficiently than ever, and the web is alive with millions of conversations and comments on brands disseminated via social media. On Facebook alone, twenty-five billion pieces of content (web links, news stories, blog posts, notes and photos) are shared every month. There are over one hundred million videos on YouTube alone. Video content, much of it on brands, is being created and disseminated by consumers, and the prospects for going viral excite marketers.

THE POWER OF USER RATINGS

Those millions of web users aren't just listening to friends; they're relying on total strangers to help them make brand choices. Product ratings have enormous sway over brand choice. Think about how many people use TripAdvisor to help them select a hotel in a city or even a particular room. The Hilton San Francisco offers guests who provide feedback to TripAdvisor free Starbucks cards, a gesture they hope will prompt a positive response. In fact, the travel industry has been turned on its head by user-generated content. Traditional standards, such as what constitutes a four-star hotel, are now determined by the public. Professional guidebooks are passé.

Marketing expert Seth Godin points out, "For the first time in history, the graffiti on the wall has more power than the official version coming from an organization (even yours)."[2] What other people say is more impor-tant than what companies say. Companies can provide information on their products, but Amazon's users will leave their own feedback. Target and Best Buy have thrown open the door for consumers to share their thoughts in fo-rums. Consumers even provide advice on how to get the most out of these companies' products—crowd sourcing at its best. Restaurant-review pub-lisher Zagats was one of the first companies to harness user-generated con-tent and share it through its annually produced books.

The amplification of the consumer voice, independent of either the media filter or the company PR department, has led to fierce internal debate at some companies about how much to let go, how much free rein to give users to have their say. Frito-Lay's Doritos believed the answer was to in-volve customers, who in turn sent great ideas that were later turned into a Super Bowl commercial.

Frank Rose in an article in the *Wall Street Journal* described it as "the Internet . . . arm[ing] the consumer against the mindless blather of corpo-rate messaging attempts."[3] Bloggers aren't paid to fill space; they're passion-ate about their topics, and they drive an honest dialogue. In some ways they have flipped the purchase funnel. Consumers can join in any web conversa-tion about brands simply by Googling the topic.

Seth Godin observed that Google has sliced and diced information about the world into tiny bits. Very few people visit a website home page anymore. They walk in the back door, the page that Google has sent them to. By atomizing the world, Google destroyed the end-to-end solution offered by most organizations, replacing it with a pick-and-choose, component-based solution. In short, they have democratized product information.[4]

ADVERTISING PROMOTES WORD OF MOUTH

Research by the Keller Fay Group found that a stunning 3.3 billion word-of-mouth brand impressions take place in the United States each day.[5] No-tably, 65 percent of brand references are positive and 8 percent negative. Looking at that statistic from a marketer's perspective, it's hard to see any downside in promoting word of mouth online. The risk is low and the upside is high. According to Keller Fay's statistics, 57 percent rated word of mouth as credible or believable and 49 percent were likely to pass on information. Advertising in traditional media has a huge role in driving word of mouth. The company found that 22 percent of daily conversations about brands, or 716 million, involves someone talking about what they'd seen or heard in paid media. In fact, the group says this is a conservative estimate of advertising's role because it counts only conversations in which ads were specifically mentioned. So it would not account for occasions when a consumer was indirectly or unconsciously motivated by an ad in a conversation about a product or service.

These findings are important, because in most research I've found that consumers don't like to admit that they're influenced by advertising. Much of the enthusiasm for word of mouth, as a communication discipline that can be molded, stems from its being more likely to be viewed as authentic and stimulated by real experience. That in itself is more valuable than paid commercial messaging.

With 22 percent of word of mouth driven by advertising and 13 percent driven by editorial content, we see that the media is playing a bigger role in driving word of mouth.[6]

WHO ARE THE INFLUENCERS?

One question marketers and agencies must ask is, Who are the influencers? The Word of Mouth Marketing Association (WOMMA) identified five broad categories of influencers (figure 6.2).[7]

BUSINESS DECISION MAKERS AND OPINION LEADERS

The viewpoint of those in formal positions of authority—political leaders or business elite, the so-called C suite, or C level—carries weight, if not final decision making, particularly on B2B products or services. But their influence also extends to credibility outside their own organizations.

FIGURE 6.2

Five Types of Influencers			
Category	Who They Are	Channels of Influence	What They Are Called (partial list)
Formal position of authority	Political/government leaders and staff; business leaders	Laws and regulations; decision and spending authority; top-down directives	Opinion leaders; decision makers; business elite
Institutional/recognized subject matter experts and advocates	Academics/scientists; industry analysts; NGO leaders; consumer activists	Academic journals; traditional media; new media; social media	Experts; mavens; analysts; critics
Media elite	Journalists; commentators; talk show hosts	Traditional media; new media; social media	Talking heads; columnists; politicos
Cultural elite	Celebrities; designers; artists; musicians	Traditional media; new media; new styles/products; social media	Trendsetters; fashionistas; taste makers; creators; starters
Socially connected	Neighborhood leaders; members of community groups; online networkers; business networkers	Personal relationships; email lists; social gatherings; social networking websites; social media	Mavens; starters; connectors; soccer moms; spreaders; hubs; alpha moms

Note: NGO, nongovernmental organization.   Source: WOMMA Influencer Handbook, 2008

2 RECOGNIZED EXPERTS AND ANALYSTS

Experts include academics, industry commentators and technical experts, people whose jobs or reputations in a specialist field put them in a position to influence others. Seth Godin is my guru on many things marketing.

3 MEDIA ELITE

Journalists, media commentators, even talk show hosts who have an audience in traditional, new or social media are the media elite. Oprah Winfrey, with her superpowers in selling books or safe driving or anything else she wants, epitomizes the type.

4 CULTURAL ELITE

Celebrities, trendsetters or fashionistas influence through their connections to pop culture and societal trends. This group is followed by early adopters and by the media. They need not necessarily be experts in a field, but they have general influence; one such is Michelle Obama.

⑤ SOCIALLY CONNECTED

Malcolm Gladwell called them mavens: everyday influencers among our family and friends—the most influential touch point.[8] They have more power than Oprah or Michelle because of their sheer number. They are researchers who are always on the lookout for new information and ideas. They volunteer their opinions about products and services they are passionate about. They are the social oil of any group, the ones with five-hundred-plus friends on Facebook who constantly socialize off- and online.

A study by ICOM, a division of direct marketing agency Epsilon, found that there is no universal influencer and that consumers are influencers strictly within product categories rather than across all categories. In addition, few commonalities exist within demographics for influencers.[9]

Each of the groups of influencers has a different role and level of importance among individual brand briefs. Each requires a different strategy. The first step is to identify and prioritize the important groups in any influencer outreach, and what you want to achieve with them, before determining tactics. We go into specifics later in this chapter in "Generating Brand Conversation Tactics."

EARLY ADOPTERS

When it comes to generating positive word of mouth, early adopters of new products are influential. The early adopters sway the "early majority," a group defined by social scientist Everett Rogers in *Diffusion of Innovations*.[10] The early majority represents 34 percent of consumers and is the group most essential for driving product sales into mainstream volume levels. According to an *Advertising Age* white paper, "Thanks to the rise of social media, early adopters have the potential to have greater influence over products they buy and try."[11]

Taly Weiss, founder and chief executive officer of Trendspotting.com Research, observed that early adopters, in the last five years, have a stage to influence others from. She says, "Social media gave them screen power. Early social media users have grown to be the important influencers, and their influence is far beyond technology."[12]

Google has exploited early adopters when developing new products such as Google Voice and Google Wave. A limited number of identified early adopters are invited by Google to test beta versions of a product. Word spreads to a growing and connected tech community, who feel they are part of an exclusive club.

Creating conversations among influencers and early adopters brings a high level of involvement for new and existing brands. Opinions of friends and family, and even those of strangers, carry more weight than company-provided information, as they are seen as independent and authentic. Social media enables spreading these opinions and discussions across a wider audience. Google and other search engines have given consumers the ability to solicit those opinions, making word of mouth more penetrating. All of this at internet speed. Building consumer conversations into the Brand Media Strategy has become a crucial element to delivering the full arsenal of paid and unpaid media communications.

TACTICS FOR GENERATING BRAND CONVERSATION

The job of the communications planner in conjunction with the marketer is to find ways to tap into those influencers and early adopters. The key tactics to keep in mind are the following:

- Start by listening.
- Talk to the talkers.
- Conversations start with an idea.
- Make it worthwhile to share.
- Amplify the conversation in paid media.
- Budget for production and ideas.
- Measure sensibly.

START BY LISTENING

As a kid I used to watch a famous British television talk show host, Michael Parkinson. He had the most engaging interviews with guests. He was renowned for not talking but listening, and he seemed to always get his guests to reveal innermost thoughts and feelings, creating fascinating conversations. During the seventies he attracted former big-name Hollywood stars such as Jimmy Stewart, John Wayne and Mickey Rooney. He didn't invite them to talk about a movie but to simply chat. In the March 4, 2006, episode, Tony Blair, the first prime minister in office to be interviewed on the show, told of his wife's father asking him if he could light a marijuana joint.

The most effective way to start a conversation is to listen. Listening can provide insight into pop culture, provide unedited thoughts about brands and what people think, in real time. There are many ways to listen. A good place for a planner to start is to set up a Google Alert for your brand and key business terms. You might want to also set up alerts to track the competition. Then analyze conversations. What are people saying? Who's saying it, how often and where and in which communities? Are views positive or negative?

Search engines have a hard time picking up commentary on chat boards, so it's important to look for forums in such places as Chow.com if you're in the restaurant business or Edmunds.com if you're working on an automotive brand. Join Facebook Groups to hear what people are saying about your client's brand. Search for URLs at Delicious.com, a site that shows who is linking to whom and where else they're going. Search.twitter.com is a place that lets you scan Twitter in real time for conversations happening around specific keywords.

A plethora of social listening tools automate brand mentions and rank them by volume, influence and sentiment. Many of them are free. We detail a number of these in chapter 12, "Measurement and Metrics."

Managing Negative Word of Mouth Online
One of the advantages of listening to the conversation online is the ability to respond.

Pepsi experienced some of the pitfalls of the online medium when an ad appeared in Germany that featured the last calorie of a drink committing suicide. The agency that made the ad had wanted to submit it for an awards program but never got Pepsi's final sign-off on the ad, so the agency ran the ad just once in a niche arts magazine in Germany. Despite the agency's caution, the copy still turned up on the web, causing immediate uproar. "Immediately we jumped in," says Bonin Bough, director of global social media at Pepsi. "We were very clear with the public that the ad will never run again, and here's how it got out; this is what the issue was."[13]

The marketing team also responded individually to all the consumers who were offended and thus helped offset damage. Taking such a transparent, honest approach can even provide "an opportunity to change a badvocate, into a potential advocate," says Bough, as long as communications are authentic and sincere.[14]

Domino's Pizza also had damage control to do after a fake video by renegade employees leaked onto YouTube. Company chief executive officer Patrick Doyle responded within twenty-four hours with his own video on YouTube.

Twitter's Trending Topics offers a way to monitor the zeitgeist and respond. When someone complains about your brand on the site, a marketer can listen or offer to help the complainer. When Matthew Caldecutt vented his frustrations with AT&T's service on his Twitter feed, AT&T wrote back to him and helped him get a better deal on his service. Caldecutt followed up with a tweet that said the company's rapid response had "turned his ill will into goodwill."[15]

TALK TO THE TALKERS

Engage Your True Fans

Marketing blogger Seth Godin talks about the shift in the conversation from how many to whom. Similarly, the president of the UK's Word of Mouth Marketing Association, Molly Flatt, says, "Your biggest spending customer may not necessarily be your most valuable. It's the one that recommends you the most that is a real asset to your business."[16] And as President Obama can attest, getting fans to convert their peers can turn a campaign into a success.

True word of mouth is most effective when it's generated by independent, peer-to-peer contact. This is the kind of behavior that brands should foster, although it demands an ethical rigor, creativity and abdication of control that can feel very frightening. Forrester Research concluded that only 16 percent of consumers trust corporate blogs, while 60 percent trust consumer product ratings and reviews.[17]

Employees Are an Advertising Medium

Sergio Zyman suggests that employees are forms of advertising. "There are plenty of times when a TV commercial is the best thing, but there are also a ton of other ways to advertise that don't involve hiring a frustrated and expensive Hollywood director," writes Zyman. "Your packaging, the way you treat your employees, the way they treat your customers, how your receptionist answers the phone, how your delivery people are dressed. Whether you care to admit it or not, all of these are advertising."[18]

In an era of web transparency, how your employees think and talk about your company has become even more crucial. Mike Kust, CMO for Carlson Marketing, noted the example of a large commercial bank that had a different message for employees and for its customers. The bank provided employees with incentives to work quicker and more efficiently, while its advertising stressed the warmth and care and extra time it gave its customers. "The whole project ended up a failure," he said.[19]

Eric Ryan, founder of the company that makes the cleaning product Method, says an employee is a spokesperson. "We blur the lines between who we are and who we serve," he says.[20] Think of your human resources director as a marketing director.

Pepsi recognized the importance of bringing its employees along, launching "invertising" for its "Refresh Everything" campaign, aimed at employees. The company placed posters, floor and elevator decals and placards in the head office in Purchase, New York. The beverage giant conducted ten webinars for its employees and bottlers that introduced the new messaging. The company also explained the plans in the company newsletter and on its intranet.

CASE STUDY: *THE DARK KNIGHT*— ENGAGING YOUR TRUE FANS

Warner Bros. showed a lot of deft in creating buzz behind *The Dark Knight* film by launching its viral marketing campaign online. The campaign launched a year before the release. They developed an elaborate Batman universe that entailed a series of interactive experiences, competitions and story builds, including more than thirty different *Dark Knight* websites. *Dark Knight* fans who went to WhySoSerious.com found themselves invited to a scavenger-hunt challenge with instructions that sent them to bakeries in 25 different US cities. After asking for an order left for "Robin Banks" ("robbing banks"), they were given a cake with a phone number written on it. Inside the cake was an evidence bag that contained a cellphone and a Joker playing card with more clues.

There was a website of the fictional newspaper *The Gotham Times*, a site for Gotham City's district attorney, Harvey Dent, suitably defaced by the Joker, and even a site for the subway map of Gotham City. These sites were not promoted through traditional media channels. They released information about them, to allow true fans to search for them and let their friends know. The film opened with a record number of screens and a record box office of $158.4 million on opening weekend in the United States.[21]

The campaign delivered some impressive numbers helped by the buzz driven by this effort: 50 million Google searches for "The Dark Knight."[22] There were 55,000 videos on YouTube tagged "The Dark Knight," with some receiving over 4 million views and generating hundreds of thousands of comments. There were 106,299 blog posts on the launch day of the film. More than 4 million websites referred to "The Dark Knight," ranging from film critics to social networks and new forums. This was a unique campaign that truly engaged the fans and drove a massive outcome.

Product more impt.

CONVERSATIONS START WITH AN IDEA

Whether you are developing campaigns that drive conversations in social or in traditional media, you need to start with an idea, a hook, something that is worth talking about and sharing. This isn't just about a media plan. Developing consumer-driven communications absolutely relies on collaborating and partnering ideas with PR and creative or digital agencies.

The more progressive ad agencies are building buzz as a central part of how they develop ad campaigns. One agency that seems to have turned this into an art form is Droga5. In 2006 they created a video for the clothing company Ecko depicting a shadowy figure breaking into Andrews Air Force Base and spray painting the words "Still Free" on the side of Air Force One. The ad was a viral sensation. In 2008 Droga5 released "Bike Hero," an ad for Activision's popular game Guitar Hero. The ad was widely praised and blogged across the internet when it was realized who its creators were.

Sometimes a creative advertising idea might have a word-of-mouth element to it. In other cases a word-of-mouth idea might be originated for the brand. To develop brand conversation ideas, planners need to do the following:

- Look for insights that could trigger effective consumer advocacy or conversations about the brand or campaign. These could come from observations of what consumers think of the brand or category in particular or from the culture in general.
- Brainstorm a single message around something that is relevant and differentiating. Is there an idea that will surprise consumers or challenge their current thinking about the brand? What is the psychological, social or cultural tension associated with this idea? What makes your target person tense about the idea? Then test the idea by asking whether she would want to share it with those she knows.

After some of these concepts have been outlined, then advertising can work to fuel a discussion, such as that prompted by Dove's "Real Beauty" campaign: "What does it mean to be beautiful?" Your ideas need to prompt a positive discussion around your brand.

FOSTER CHICKENS—SAY NO TO PLUMPING

Foster Farms, in Livingston, California, launched an online marketing campaign that caught my eye.[23] The company sells high-quality chicken in supermarkets. Faced with the effect of lower-priced store brands on their sales, they came up with a brilliant idea that challenged their current approach to purchase consideration by bringing to light the practices of lower-priced competitor products. They did this by creating an issue-based campaign to "Say no to plumping."

Plumping, a word invented by Foster Farms, describes the practice, largely unknown to consumers, of filling chickens with saltwater to make them heavier. The heavier the chicken, the more you pay. Foster Farms wanted to explain why its chickens were worth the money.

Foster Farms, together with design consultancy Welikesmall and ad agency Goodby, Silverstein & Partners, San Francisco, California, designed a website to discuss the evils of the practice. A YouTube ad spot shows a shady surgeon injecting chicken characters who don't understand what's going on. The antiplumping campaign has its own website, Twitter address and Facebook page. The idea sparked so much interest that even California senator Barbara Boxer got involved to suggest that producers label chickens that have been injected with saltwater.[24]

Another technique is to create an event worth talking about, and publish, broadcast and promote it in paid and earned media platforms to help drive conversations. John Woodward, in charge of global planning at Publicis, advocates creating what he calls "contagious ideas that change the conversation."[25]

For New Zealand beer Speights, their idea was to sponsor an event and then PR and promote it. The agency built a Speights ale house on a ship that made a ten-week voyage to London, where it then served expat Kiwis who missed their favorite drink. Footage of the voyage was sent to websites, the media and television. The huge media interest generated PR with a value of millions of dollars over several months, a value that was many times the brand's original promotional budget.

MAKE IT WORTH THEIR WHILE TO SHARE

Every PR person knows that giving a journalist an exclusive—a piece of information, a story or access—will most likely lead to a sense of excitement and a desire to share.

Potato snack Pringles, a Procter & Gamble product, launched a campaign with this idea in mind. Their approach was to share a new product with a group of people who might then go out and spread the word. Pringles distributed a first-to-taste party pack that was sent to networked mothers in advance of a traditional media launch. It invited snack food influencers to have their friends taste and rate the new Rice Infusion brand of Pringles. This produced a flurry of conversations about the product, both on- and offline.

Bloggers love recognition, so give them access to your brands. To bring these influencers into the tent, it's critical to have them interact with the product, rate it and then talk about it, both positively and negatively. Consumer electronics company Panasonic invited influential bloggers on a trip to the Consumer Electronics Show in Las Vegas, Nevada, where they mingled with Panasonic's chief executive officer and marketing people. They didn't insist that anyone write about the product, but they did receive plenty of buzz in the end.

Our UK office, working with mobile phone operator O2, gave college students prizes to promote the mobile phone company's unlimited use for a flat rate plan. The big prize was an end-of-term party for the winner's entire university. Some 250 student brand ambassadors were appointed to spread the word face to face and through their social networks. The student awareness of the rate plan doubled, going from 21 percent to 43 percent. The phone company also showed an average increase of 77 percent over all brand attributes among students for the campaign period.

Similarly, Pepsi's Refresh project taps into consumers' deep desire to do good and to be connected to each other while doing so. "Refresh" aims to give away millions of dollars to good causes. Those looking for cash to support their initiatives are required to launch a political-like campaign within their on- and offline social networks to get people to vote for their initiative.

In July 2010, Pepsi's project, at www.refresheverything.com, had 1,086 pitches from consumers in categories such as health, arts, food, the planet, neighborhood and education.[26] Voters could support anything from free crock pots and recipes for the underprivileged to Kindle classrooms for those wanting to learn English.

The YouTube Effect

YouTube has helped agencies to create viral communications for their clients. In the 2008 Effie Awards, YouTube featured in fifty-five of the ninety-four winning campaigns.[27]

Creating desirable content is the key to having that content shared. But there are also clever strategies to exploit YouTube's ubiquity and mass reach. Gaming-console maker Nintendo wanted to persuade a broader family audience to play and bought the YouTube home page to premiere its ad. That resulted in "one million click-throughs in three days," according to Nintendo.[28]

AMPLIFY THE CONVERSATION IN PAID MEDIA

As mentioned earlier, according to Keller Fay, at least 22 percent of word-of-mouth conversations about brands are generated by advertising. And many of those conversations are positive to the brand. Building in paid media strategies that fuel brand conversations is more essential than ever.

Airline JetBlue is a classic example of how to build a brand on word of mouth. Approximately 70 percent of their customers fly with the airline because someone has recommended JetBlue. The company wanted to amplify the voices of those satisfied customers and set up a story booth. Customers were asked to share their story in person in the booth or online. The JetBlue booth was taken to eleven cities, and over 109,000 people stopped in to talk. The company collected over one thousand video stories and over twelve hundred emails. The stories from the booth formed the basis for a television ad campaign and a twenty-minute video shown on planes and in crew member areas to help drive the culture.

The outcome was that travelers gave greater consideration to JetBlue when making flight plans than to rivals such as Southwest, 26 percent versus 23 percent, respectively, for the two airlines. The company's revenue, passenger and miles were up 25 percent.[29]

Super Bowl Has Become the PR Bowl

Ed Keller, chief executive officer of Keller Fay Group, firmly believes that the Super Bowl generates substantially more word of mouth for advertisers than anything else out there. "We generally see that brands which advertise in the Super Bowl are rewarded with a 15% increase in Word of Mouth. . . . This translates into more than 100 million incremental conversations for advertised brands in the week after the game than the average weekly Word of Mouth they were realizing previously." Keller figures that a word-of-mouth conversation is worth about fifty cents to a marketer and that there's a social value being generated that goes beyond the impact of the ad itself.[30]

This came to life for me when my agency worked with Denny's. In an effort to gain retrial and increase brand consideration, they developed a promotion to invite America to have a Denny's Grand Slam breakfast free of charge.

On Super Bowl Sunday we timed the release of our in-game spot, digital campaign and brand website takeover to launch simultaneously. Denny's became the most talked about restaurant in America in less than forty hours. The campaign delivered incredible buzz. It was the second-most-searched word on Super Bowl Sunday and the number-one tweeted subject on Twitter that day.

Denny's leveraged news and trade media on the Monday after the big game. Over two thousand television stations and five hundred newspapers covered our story. Thousands of websites and over ten thousand blogs helped propagate Denny's advertising message all over Facebook, YouTube and Twitter.

The campaign generated fifty million dollars in free media exposure as the press and television picked up the feel-good story of a free Denny's breakfast in the midst of a gloomy recession. It drove significant consideration and retrial.

Leveraging Specialist Word-of-Mouth
and Media Partners to Amplify Brand Conversations

Sometimes media companies can really help drive word of mouth and interest for a brand. To dramatically boost sales of Garnier Nutritioniste Eye Rollers, my agency focused on using media partners to speak to key influencers and drive product recommendation.

The program built word of mouth in a few ways but most directly through a partnership with SheSpeaks, a network of over fifty thousand female opinion drivers who were invited to participate in sampling and share their experience with others.

To begin, we invited two thousand SheSpeaks panelists within the Eye Roller's target age group of twenty-five to thirty-five years old to participate in the test. The panelists took part in an online survey to enroll in the Eye Roller program. Once enrolled, program participants were sent a sample of the Eye Roller, along with access to an online microsite with detailed product information and online coupons for panelists to use and pass along. The women provided feedback and participated in an interactive discussion about the Eye Roller in a discussion forum. At the end of the program, participants were invited to take an evaluation survey to provide feedback about the Eye Roller and to share their experiences with others about the product. Women-targeted magazines such as *Cookie*, *Allure* and *Self* were also asked to share the product with their most active readers and asked to discuss their experience through online forums.

Of the magazine readers who tried the product, 86 percent said they were likely to recommend the product. Those reached through the SheSpeaks program increased purchase intent 174 percent. The outcome was unprecedented. The Garnier Nutritioniste Eye Roller sold over one million products in the first six months of the program, and those sales helped move the entire Garnier Nutritioniste franchise into the top five skincare companies in 2008.

BUDGET FOR PRODUCTION AND IDEAS

Traditionally, word-of-mouth campaigns are funded from marketing, public relations, promotions, events or digital budgets. Rarely are they part of the media plan's budget, such is the lack of integration that still besets our industry. Marketing PR is someone else's responsibility. But that way of thinking is being challenged by the media agencies.

Word-of-mouth programs are not a media buy, but they can and should be incorporated into the communications plan. The cost is primarily in development of the creative ideas, project management of the campaign and various production or technology areas in the case of social media programs. If you have an idea or recommendation for a word-of-mouth program, the best way to make it possible is to include a provision in the media budget. Even though that budget may not be placed with paid media vendors, the outcome is about creating brand exposure and influence.

MEASURE SENSIBLY

Be careful about measuring word of mouth, because it can't be treated the same way other media metrics are. Word of mouth is about influencing others rather than being a traditional headcount.

Some metrics are used as basic benchmarks of word of mouth. Many of them are collected through social media monitoring or general market surveys. The general metrics measured will include page views, volume of posts, people reached, comments on posts, sentiment shifts and number of fans. These are useful reference points to quantify reach and fine-tune the tactics. But in the end many effective social media tactics are the most difficult to measure quantitatively. Measuring the holistic key performance indicators (KPIs) of the Brand Media Strategy is the end game. We will cover this in chapter 12.

QUESTIONS WHEN DEVELOPING
BRAND CONVERSATION TACTICS

1. What communication goals do you want to achieve?
2. Who are the most important influencers for this brand or campaign?
3. Will the idea surprise consumers or challenge their current thinking about the brand?
4. What will make them want to share it?
5. What touch points will reach and amplify the idea best?

CHAPTER 7

CONDUCTING
THE ORCHESTRA

MAKING INTEGRATION REAL

O ne of the toughest acts to pull off in marketing is integration. It's the ultimate goal for all campaigns, because it's critical to ensuring a more complete consumer experience. But integration is hard to achieve. Only 25 percent of advertisers report that they are doing integrated marketing "very well" or "excellent," down from 33 percent in 2006.[1]

Integration is difficult for a lot of reasons. Agencies are splintered into specialist fields: creative, media and digital, but other channels from shopper marketing to sponsorship are also part of the marketing communications mix. Agencies don't have financial incentives to work together. As agencies naturally strive to preserve their fees, this works against integration. And in this era of accountability, agencies and measurement want to distill the performance of individual pieces of the marketing communications puzzle.

This chapter covers two ideas:

1. What it takes to make integration work on the agency side
2. How to make the Brand Media Strategy come together so consumers receive a holistic brand experience

MAKING MUSIC IN COMMUNICATIONS

Although never much of a music buff, my interest swelled when my two sons started playing in their middle school band. Attending my boys' concerts, I've noticed that music has some lessons for us about integration in the advertising business.

An orchestra is made up of different specialists: percussion, woodwind, brass and strings. In our case, advertising has an ensemble of creative, media, digital, PR and other agencies. Each section in its own right is special, but playing together in harmony creates an amazing performance. Everyone plays to the same music and in the same meter, but each instrument has its own arrangement. If all the instruments played the same tune at the same time, the performance would be flat, one dimensional. If each section were to play its own tune, it would be cacophony. Each instrument has its moment to shine, but the overall vision of the arrangement is the hero, not led by or defaulting to any single instrument. I wonder how harmonious the multiple agencies working together on a campaign sound to the client?

RETHINKING INTEGRATION

Working together in harmony, the most rudimentary point of integration, is often violated, most painfully when digital elements are added as an afterthought.

Gone are the days when creative solely drove everything; so too are the days when media led the campaign. And digital ruling it all isn't the answer either. Everyone has to come together, play their part.

There's a growing need for better integration given the increase in media usage. Among entries to the Institute of Practitioners in Advertising Effectiveness Awards, television remains the dominant medium, used in twenty-two of the twenty-three winners.[2] That's unsurprising, given television's still unrivalled ability to bring reach and impact for mass-market brands. What is changing is the way television is blended with other channels. Last year's winners used on average six different media channels; in 2004, four; in 1990, two. The number of available channels has exploded, and there is clearly a corresponding cultural shift from using a single channel or a single marketing discipline toward a blending of many tools. Media-led solutions are increasingly evident. As agencies evolve, so too does campaign development. Clients demand a more synthesized approach. Figure 7.1 illustrates the shifts agencies are making to bring about a more integrated approach to a Brand Media Strategy.

In the mass media era, the modus operandi at many ad agencies was first to crack the creative idea. Media plans were developed in parallel, but little could be finalized until the creative was determined. That creative idea usually came in the form of either a thirty-second television ad or a print ad. It was assumed that these media would carry the campaign to most of the target consumers.

Once sign-off by the client was obtained, the creative teams would develop other media executions—radio, digital display and below-the-line tactics such as direct marketing and point of sale. There would be room for some creative media ideas, perhaps ads printed on tomatoes or zany out-of-home executions for the purposes of award entries. Digital usually took

FIGURE 7.1

A Shift in Developing Communications		
Mass Media Era		Today
Creative ideas established first, then media plan developed	➡	Branding idea/Communications Planning established ahead of creative
The big TV idea	➡	The big communications idea
Full-service agencies	➡	Specialist agencies collaborating
30-second TV, full-page print ads	➡	Content in multiple platforms
Multimedia strategy	➡	Multichannel strategy

another path, often through another agency and another manager in the client company. It would be unkind and inaccurate to say this happened all the time, but it would equally be untrue to say it happened only occasionally. The better agency teams wouldn't let that happen, but for many, deadlines, pragmatism and legacy practices caused the process to fall back on bad habits.

Rob Feakins, chief creative officer and president at Publicis, New York, illustrates the new order. While working on a new business assignment, he charged several teams in his creative department to come up with a campaign. Before the teams presented their ideas to him, he called me and asked if I could talk him through the communications plan. I was intrigued; rarely does creative express much interest in the media plan. I asked him why he needed this. He said the relative importance of different media would help him judge the potential campaign concepts better. Knowing whether out-of-home or print or television advertising was going to be the principal channel would help him decide which idea to back.

Clearly, a shift is taking place. With a need for media-neutral strategies, we can't assume that television will always be the lead medium. Today, it makes more sense to start with understanding how and where we would connect with the target consumer and how we should use the media before we determine what to say. However, I don't think that this is a one-way process. A good Brand Media Strategy needs to be validated and challenged by those responsible for executing it. Media and creative is a partnership.

THE BIG TELEVISION IDEA VERSUS THE BIG COMMUNICATIONS IDEA

The big television idea in advertising has lost ground to small, smartly placed, relevant impressions. Media's long tail requires that we look at not just mass audience but a broader combination of touch points. Single media campaigns these days are rare, because planners need to deploy several media to deliver sufficient reach. Often heavy online users will be light television viewers and vice versa, so each medium needs to promote the campaign as if it was the primary one. In chapter 2, I described in the New Media Playbook section the importance of using communication to create involvement and relevancy. Central to that is considering how each medium is consumed and the different relationships and experiences that consumers have with each medium, and then exploiting those qualities. For example, when Activision promoted Guitar Hero 5, its television commercial, which played heavily in football programming, was designed to stand out among the heavy football and male-skewed commercials; its social media programs contained a lot of fan participation and interaction; and its teaser campaign on YouTube had very little branding and more risqué humor that encouraged viral pass-on.

As communications agencies, we want to avoid the matching-luggage syndrome or the "let's replicate the print into banners and TV into radio" urge. That's why a campaign needs a strategic platform or a big communications idea to help bring the campaign together.

At Optimedia, we call this the central communicating idea, or CCI. I've heard different agencies describe it as the brand or big idea, or the strategic or connections platform. Its purpose is to ensure that all the communications across the multiple channels are on message, appropriate to the target and strategic. The CCI allows us to anchor and integrate the Brand Media Strategy and the media activations.

The CCI should inspire creativity. It is not the creative tagline or the ad, but it can incorporate or leverage the creative idea. It is channel agnostic and allows multiple tactics and executions to be activated. It should lead the briefing process for activation opportunities across the different marketing communications disciplines. We develop the CCI in collaboration with different specialists—creative, digital, direct, broadcast, print, out-of-home and emerging media in a series of workshops.

Axe body spray's CCI is "The magic promise of mating game success." This idea straddles the advertising, different media executions and marketing touch points. The television ads sell this idea in thirty seconds. It was expanded with a branded television series about young men's quests to win women. Another addition to this was the playful Axe mating-game tool kit, which users could access online. The idea was masterfully executed with creativity and by exploiting individual media's different strengths but all selling the same broad idea. That's the orchestra effect in advertising.

THE BIG IDEA DRIVES INTEGRATION

The CCI should open the door to many tactics and be able to travel across many media platforms in multiple countries. It ensures all marketing communications work together in harmony. It calls for thinking collaboratively and connecting all agencies to provide integrated, focused communications execution. Once you have a CCI then work with the partners to develop media solutions and tactics.

IS THE CENTRAL COMMUNICATING IDEA
THE ACTUAL CREATIVE IDEA?

The CCI should in most cases be interchangeable with the creative idea or core brand idea.

The obvious place to start is with the campaign's creative idea. The role of the Brand Media Strategy could be to amplify that idea across all media effectively. I'm not the kind of planner who thinks that media insights and ideas have to be developed separately from the creative process. Leveraging the creative idea is a powerful and proven strategy that delivers integration.

Rather than describe a solution as integrated, we should think of it as unifying a concept that brings a lot of different ideas, tactics and executions together in a meaningful, cohesive way. The Pepsi MAX "Wake Up People!" campaign highlights this superbly.

DEVELOP A CENTRAL COMMUNICATIONS IDEA FIRST,
THEN THE CREATIVE

The CCI is developed from a consumer insight or truth that is relevant to the target audience we want to influence. Ideally, the direction helps determine how you use media to differentiate the brand from the competition.

CASE STUDY: PEPSI "WAKE UP PEOPLE!"[3]

The challenge was to introduce a diet cola, Diet Pepsi MAX, into an already overcrowded marketplace, containing some 150 energy drinks.

The objective was to maximize and repeat trial over an initial four-month launch period. The campaign idea was to wake up tired consumers, who were identified by their yawns. The idea behind this campaign launch for an energy drink containing double the caffeine and ginseng was to deliver energy to the masses.

The highly contagious, inappropriate yawn was used as a visual device across a fully integrated television, radio, out-of-home, internet and PR guerrilla campaign. The central communicating idea was "Stop the yawn."

The campaign to "Stop the yawn" began a national crusade against afternoon slumps and daily exhaustion. Television drove awareness of the advertising creative, which featured yawns getting people into trouble. Diet Pepsi MAX ambassadors set up Wake-up stations in malls, festivals, offices, tourist attractions and commuter locations in major cities around the United States.

The events targeted busy commuters and shoppers throughout their day. They created minigames that reinforced the idea. For example, Whack-a-Yawn, a take on the classic Whack-a-Mole carnival game, allowed consumers to hammer their yawns away with a mallet shaped like a Diet Pepsi MAX can. In Stop-the-Yawn video game arcades, consumers used MAX water guns to squirt yawns away. These activities became major sampling events, with more than five hundred thousand samples handed out. Consumers also had the chance to view the latest television ads.

The campaign resulted in a greater number of household trials than did any other launch by Pepsi or rival Coke in the previous eighteen months. Brand awareness and persuasion were 17 percent higher than the category norms.

Sometimes the CCI can lead the communications campaign and shape the creative approach. The Mars Galaxy Chocolate UK campaign is a great example of this.

CASE STUDY: MARS GALAXY CHOCOLATE, UK[4]

Galaxy sought to become part of the indulgence rituals that enrich women's lives.

The insight: that millions of women entered a richly imaginative world when reading books. Sixty percent of women indulge their passion for reading every week. And reading books was an increasingly common pastime among women. Chocolate and reading were guilty pleasures that went hand in hand, so the marketer attempted to create relationships to exploit that partnership.

Galaxy, over a three-year period, developed a relationship with women via the indulgence of reading. The strategy started as 15 percent of the activation budget and has developed into the mainstay of brand communications, inviting women to "unwind with a good book."

Galaxy built partnerships with publishers and with UK television presenters Richard and Judy, who had a talk show featuring book selections. Galaxy also worked with retailers such as supermarkets and bookstores. The deals with publishers meant that around 26 million books carried the Galaxy brand on the front cover. Galaxy sponsored book clubs, the product appeared inside and on the covers of books, and ads were adjacent to book displays.

Galaxy also sponsored the British Book Awards, in which the public votes. As a result of the campaign, in a tough sales environment Galaxy won its biggest market share in 2008: 17.9 percent. Galaxy enjoyed a 38 percent rise in sales over the previous year, compared to an 8 percent rise for rival Cadbury's Dairy Milk.

We will explore how to develop CCIs in chapter 11, "Execution Is the X-Factor."

FULL-SERVICE AGENCIES VERSUS
INDEPENDENT SPECIALIST AGENCIES

In reality, very few if any truly full-service agencies exist today. The industry has evolved to the point that agencies can't possibly provide everything. It's impossible to have creative, media planning and buying, website development, online advertising, online search, events, PR, social media, packaging and shopper marketing under the same roof.

Usually, agencies provide central integrated thinking and services but bring in specialist discipline partners to support and implement the programs. Some specialist partners are managed or owned within their agency's holding company groups. Many times they are independent firms or separately appointed by the clients. Whatever the structure, what's absolutely necessary is the ability to collaborate with different departments and specialist teams. Some of these teams will have their own distinct culture or may even be competitors. An environment that unifies the teams is an important ingredient for succeeding.

BRINGING MEDIA BACK INTO THE AGENCY

This has been a source of debate in the industry. Creative agencies are missing the input of media, particularly communications planning. However, simply putting media back in the agency proves to be a challenge.

First, the media fifteen years ago was not as complicated as it is now. Today, a media Renaissance man or woman is rare. Such a person needs to not only be smart, have great relationships with media vendors and be able to work with creatives but also have strong strategic and consumer insight, have flair, be conversant with all the digital and emerging channels and have a strong aptitude for data analysis. It's rare to find all that in one person. The communications planner today relies on a team of specialists whom they can access and collaborate with.

A number of creative agencies have added communications planning to their offerings. Some have succeeded, while others have struggled to make it work. The ability for media to have a voice and influence has rested largely on the personality of the planner and on the commitment by the agency management to listen and respond to communications planning in largely account-management or creative-driven cultures.

We created Optimedia Inside to place communications planners into Publicis, to work with their clients. It became complementary to the account planning and creative development process but had the full support of the same research tools, data and specialist-channel expertise that we had back at the media agency mother ship.

COLLABORATION AND INTEGRATION APPROACHES

I am going to cite a few UK examples here because UK agencies seem to tackle collaboration and integration better. This isn't a slight on the United States or other regions, just my personal observation. Unbundled agencies and communications planning agencies have been operating in the United Kingdom longer than in many other markets, but in general, I also see a greater emphasis on planning and collaboration.

The biggest advertiser in the United Kingdom is the government, whose advertising is principally managed by the Central Office of Information (COI), a central marketing and advertising body that supports government departments in managing information campaigns in areas such as health, education, benefits, rights and welfare.

The COI has a unique model for collaboration: it matches up teams, placing creative and media agencies together to pitch for government business. The media agencies manage communications planning, and media buying is handled by a separate agency of record. The COI argues that they want to put the best-in-class agencies together, and it puts the onus on the agencies to partner effectively if they want to win the account.

Even if an agency holding company has all the necessary expertise, what's needed in the new communications world are great collaborative skills and shared beliefs and a common culture. In other words, they must need and want to work together. Clients should look for an agency with clearly defined roles and incentives for people to work together along with openness to each company's ideas and opinions.

Speaking at the American Advertising Federation 2009 annual meeting, Tracy Benson, senior director of marketing and digital at Best Buy, said, "We need to talk about our brands, across a number of touch points."[5] To adjust to such integration, she said, the first requirement is "a shift in mindset of every agency employee. There can be no boundaries." An integrated marketing program must focus on "what's best for the brand, not for me as a media specialist. You need to get creative and PR teams thinking that way."

From the agency perspective, Sarah Personette, vice president at Publicis Groupe's MediaVest Worldwide, says integration depends on three simple words: "Check your ego."

DEVELOPING T-SHAPED PEOPLE

T-shaped people combine a depth of knowledge in one marketing discipline with a breadth of understanding in the wider spectrum of disciplines. They know how each discipline can be blended with others to deliver one integrated campaign.

Ideal blends of skill sets include creative people who have an appreciation of media, digital executives who have an understanding of how branding works and media people willing to explore nontraditional solutions.

CHI & Partners managing partners Sarah Golding and Neil Goodlad claim that agencies need to be rich in creative and planning talent and media buying.[6] There's no place for tired preconceptions and complacencies in a participative world. People have to have confidence in new media. They need to learn the necessary new skills.

CONTENT ON MULTIPLE PLATFORMS

As media companies branch out by putting content on different platforms to maximize their audience potential, an agency's Brand Media Strategy needs to leverage that into opportunity.

Different platforms communicate differently, deliver different communication experiences. Creative that is developed for, rather than adapted to, the medium is going to be more relevant to how consumers interact and use that medium. For example, MasterCard's "Priceless" campaign uses television to build on the emotion of what *priceless* can mean at a very human level. In 2009 MasterCard's www.priceless.com provided great consumer-facing applications that supported the brand proposition. These include the MasterCard Gift Finder, Priceless Pointers and tools and tips for better handling credit and finances. The company created a mobile Priceless Picks application, which recognizes your location and presents a three-dimensional map of Priceless picks: recommended restaurants, bars, museums and popular items on sale.

MULTIMEDIA STRATEGY, MULTICHANNEL STRATEGY

A multimedia strategy focuses on different advertising solutions. A multichannel strategy encompasses several more drivers for marketing, for example, advertising to drive the brand, direct marketing to drive response, point of sale and packaging to drive purchase.

Traditional boundaries of media are being pushed beyond advertising as clients look for broader advice on their marketing plan. Google is as much an ecommerce driver as it is a brand tool. Social media is as much about driving PR as driving the brand. Mobile and online are as much coupon distribution tools as they are advertising tools.

Sponsorship on television and radio are comparable to sponsorship of events. As media seeks to increase experiences, agencies are going outside traditional media venues to promote brands.

NONMEDIA CHANNELS

Specialist marketing channels, such as content providers and sponsorship, are working with media agencies to target traditional media budgets, and clients want the rigor of evaluation and measurement of media platforms to be applied to other marketing channel decisions.

This is stretching communications planning into an area that many planners are less comfortable in, the area of nonmedia advertising channels. Nonmedia channels have budgets that are often double the traditional media budget.

BRINGING IT BACK TOGETHER—LIKE AN ORCHESTRA

Two key roles bring the orchestra together: those of the composer and the conductor. The composer is really the owner of the strategy. In advertising, strategy is a joint effort. There's the marketing plan, the brand idea, the Brand Media Strategy and the digital program. At the end of the day, the client has final say on how it pieces together.

Then there is the conductor. Who fills the role of conductor in a marketing campaign is largely dependent on the attitude of the client. Mark Ritson, associate professor of marketing at Melbourne Business School in Australia and a vocal spokesperson on branding globally, says that only the brand manager or client can fill this role.[7] The conductor role often defaults to the agencies. Traditionally, the creative agency has lead. However, I have seen very successful examples of the lead role being performed by the digital agency, the communications planning agency or the PR agency.

When I worked with Procter & Gamble, the strategic lead person was often the brand manager, who worked with his or her marketing service partners. Other clients have had in place an integrated marketing team, whose role is to coordinate and steer the outputs of the different agencies.

What's important is to have clear rules of engagement, a spirit of collaboration and a focus on the work. One example of how I've seen it work brilliantly is when our UK agency worked with mobile network company O2, which espoused all these qualities and epitomized them with their internal mantra "It only works if it all works."

CASE STUDY: O2 FORMULA FOR INTEGRATION

Our agency worked with an incredible client and a superb creative agency, VCCP, alongside digital shop Agency Republic and PR firm Jackie Cooper. This union represented true marketing communications integration.

O2 was one of the most celebrated integrated-brand marketing stories in the United Kingdom in the 2000s. The agency team helped transform the former British Telecom cell phone division into a power brand that differentiated itself in one of the highest-spending and most competitive categories. They grew their business from number four to number one in the market.

They knew they wanted to build their brand, but their budget needed to support both their product and promotional initiatives. The challenge for O2 was how to be successful on both counts simultaneously. The solution was to ensure complete strategic integration.

INDEPENDENT, SPECIALIST AGENCIES COLLABORATING

The client encouraged us to work together as one team and selected agency partners and teams that shared the same values, culture and passion for their brand. We all got on and had respect for each other. A lot of credit went to O2's creative agency, VCCP, which always wanted to be inclusive and integrated in media. Integrating O2's communications would be a major weapon in competing against higher-spending rivals. Integration became a necessity to be efficient and competitive.

The project began with the client chairing communications teams that included senior management from the creative, media, digital and PR agencies, who would steer their communications. This encouraged senior agency leaders to focus on the business.

BIG COMMUNICATION IDEAS

O2 took a very brand-centric approach to communicating their initiatives.

Rather than just being a provider of mobile technology or becoming a mobile visionary, O2 set out to become a brand that enabled the customer to do more things. They wanted to portray a brand that existed solely to provide the customer more ways to work, play and communicate.

This central idea of "enablement" and the company's attitude of emphasizing fresh thinking led to a kind of can-do mantra and the creation of a set of values: bold, open, trusted and clear. That was how the communications team was expected to work.

COMMUNICATIONS PLANNING AHEAD OF CREATIVE EXECUTION

O2 was a retail business that was very focused on monthly performance numbers such as new acquisitions and churn, or the number of people who leave the service.

The campaign needed to work to reinforce the brand, but most importantly it needed to work as a promotion to drive those statistics in the right direction. O2's campaign was never about advertising, but about an idea. They maximized the effectiveness of communications by integrating all the elements so that the brand idea could be carried through to each aspect of the marketing. All the agency partners had opportunities to develop multimedia executions.

O2's marketing worked because the company started with a brand idea, rather than a creative execution. That brand idea was driven by a consumer insight that helped drive communications planning. For example, when promoting free texting between 7 P.M. and 8 P.M. for new customers, they developed the promotion around the brand idea of happy hour. This manifested in different media tactics, including taxi cab advertising with O2-branded cabs offering free rides between 7 P.M. and 8 P.M. and happy hour promotions in bars and pubs.

COORDINATING A MULTICHANNEL STRATEGY

The brand idea and the can-do attitude informed and shaped everything from product positioning to advertising and sponsorship, from staff conferences to trade launches. It also enabled the business to use what typically would be short-term initiatives to fuel long-term brand growth.

Other brands in the UK phone market appeared more remote from their day-to-day product offering. Rivals established an image and a personality through their brand with product offerings, such as bonus airtime and new service plans. But they were used in a tactical way, to drive short-term sales.

O2 had neither the time nor the resources to adopt such a parallel approach. Rather than treating products as technical gizmos, or tariffs as tactical one-off promotions, O2's communications wrapped the whole company in the brand idea. This was intended not only to create consumer-focused propositions that were of genuine interest and relevance but also to drive positive associations with the brand.

O2 also understood that putting out messaging, product support or promotions across different touch points in the same period added to confusion and misappropriation, and it competed for attention and mind space. The company was very disciplined in running a single campaign in all media.

CONSISTENT BRAND LOOK

The cell phone company has benefited enormously from the efficiencies of a very complete visual integration across all communication channels, from television to print to online and in-store. The distinctive blue visual branding and the O2 bubbles and neonlike campaign elements were evident in all communication touch points.

QUESTIONS TO ASK TO
FACILITATE COMMUNICATION INTEGRATION

1. Does the campaign have a central communicating idea?
2. Can this campaign travel across multiple touch points?
3. Is there a spirit of collaboration among the agency teams?
4. Are there clear rules of engagement with the agencies?
5. Do I have T-shaped skills? If not, in what areas do I need to develop my skills?

CHAPTER 8

UNLOCKING MOMENTS
OF RECEPTIVITY

HOW MEDIA CONTEXT HELPS ADVERTISING
DELIVER MORE RELEVANT COMMUNICATIONS

In the late nineties, I worked as a media planner at Saatchi & Saatchi on the agency's prized Procter & Gamble account. At the time, I recall, our Saatchi & Saatchi New York office recommended a media strategy that proved to be a breakthrough for Tide laundry detergent.

Tide, like many brands in the Procter & Gamble portfolio back then, was primarily a television advertiser. The brand targeted the household shopper, and television efficiently delivered strong reach to the target. The problem was that the brand was beginning to plateau. The agency team took a brave step in recommending a switch in strategy.

The idea was to make Tide advertising more relevant to its audience by placing it at the point of dirt. The company shifted more of its budget to out-of-home media, and Tide ads appeared on so-called dirty media: on the back of buses above the tail pipe, in train stations, in playgrounds and at agricultural exhibitions in rural areas. Tide ads appeared on paper napkins in diners and in a variety of external city locations—each with customized creative messages. For example, they placed an ad on bus shelters near ice cream stores that said, "When your popsicle suddenly becomes just a sip. . . ." The idea was to make people think of the product when they encountered a dirty environment. Sales of Tide grew 9 percent in markets where the campaign ran.

The role of a relevant location—coupled with relevant messaging—is a powerful idea. It was a very deliberate choice of creativity above coverage, impact over efficiency. I refer to this as receptivity planning—that is, identifying the moments or places consumers will be more receptive to the messaging. It's becoming an increasingly prominent component of Brand Media Strategy.

Receptivity planning has utility beyond outdoor advertising. Technology platforms are quickly bringing this planning into this decade. We're seeing placement of, for example, online advertising based on content and well-placed links with relevant search terms. We are seeing increased opportunities for location-based advertising on mobile media and addressable advertising on television.

We will explore receptivity tactics in more depth in this chapter.

DRIVING INCREASED ENGAGEMENT

As I've noted in the preceding chapters, the job of communications planning is to influence, not just reach, people. In the ad business we're obsessed with engagement. Some agencies have established engagement planning departments. It's advertising's equivalent of Sir Lancelot's Holy Grail. The problem is that it's hard to define, hard to measure and something of a catch-all term. But engagement isn't something new. Creative directors will tell you that the purpose of an ad has always been to engage its audience. As I see it, four main factors influence marketing communications engagement.

THE BRAND OFFER OR BRAND ITSELF

A Sony flat-screen television on sale for 75 percent off will certainly get attention. On the other hand, a new product launch from Apple in itself creates instant interest. Well before anyone saw or touched an iPad, the buzz was deafening.

THE APPEAL AND IMPACT OF THE MESSAGE ITSELF

The craft and delivery of the creative execution can make a brand famous and get people interested. British chocolate company Cadbury fielded an ad campaign of a gorilla playing the drums to a Phil Collins song, "In the Air Tonight." It became a viral sensation, gaining over ten million plays on YouTube and resulting in seventy Facebook sites. The video was popular because it was different and unexpected and, in a sea of communications clutter, it engaged. Consumers talked about it and bought the company's chocolate bars.

THE MIND-SET OF THE CONSUMER

Consumers who are already looking for a product or service will be more engaged in what the advertiser is saying. If you're planning a vacation to Australia, you notice any ad or article featuring the outback or Sydney Harbor Bridge. The consumer's own lifestyle and interests stimulate interest. We know that NASCAR fans have a strong propensity toward brands that sponsor its cars or drivers.

THE CONTEXT OF THE MESSAGE:
HOW AND WHEN IS IT DELIVERED?

The context or environment the ad message appears in has a strong influence on the level of engagement. Primarily, this is about relevance: relevance to the message, relevance to the product or relevance to the consumer.

Clearly, the client, the creative agency and the media teams all play a role in determining engagement. From a media communications perspective, we center on the last two factors: the mind-set of the consumer and the context of how and when the message is delivered.

Should the communications planner have a say in the creative work itself? I say let the creative people get on with creative. They have a tough job. In this business, everyone—up to and including the chairman's spouse—is allowed to have an opinion on the ads. One of our principal roles as communications planners is to make that messaging work better and harder.

Communications planners can't determine the creative but they can deliver receptivity; the right viewers, mind-set, context. Don Gloeckler, Procter & Gamble's chief researcher in North America, observes, "I am less able to influence engagement than I am able to influence receptivity."[1] Engagement is an outcome of receptivity. The best communications planner knows how to exploit media that seeks out the most receptive consumer.

WHAT DO WE MEAN BY RECEPTIVITY?

Receptivity is about shifting from *delivering* messages to understanding how they are *received.* It is about focusing on context: finding the most relevant places to match the media with the message, the consumer with the brand. Receptivity is concerned with using media to drive brand and message involvement. Most importantly, it concerns generating deeper impressions, not just gross impressions.

IT'S NEVER BEEN ABOUT REACHING EVERYONE

Brand Media Strategies that concentrate on mass-audience reach as the principal driver of generating more sales are no longer effective. That approach is expensive and unreliable.

To give an idea of how blunt traditional broad targeting can be, let's look at auto giant Toyota, an extensive media advertiser. Sales of its best-selling Camry at the peak of the market had annual US sales of 400,000 to 450,000 cars. Typically, an agency might plan and buy for a demographic of men and women aged twenty-five to fifty-four with a household income above seventy-five thousand dollars. That target demographic accounts for some fifty-seven million. So in this case, less than 1 percent of the people targeted were in the market to buy.

Reaching fewer people more efficiently is one of the principles guiding our approach to receptivity planning.

RECEPTIVITY PLANNING IS NOT
PUTTING ADS NEXT TO RELEVANT CONTENT

Some people may think receptivity is about running ads for food products in the cooking section of women's magazines or placing car ads on automotive websites such as Edmunds.com. That isn't what's meant. These environments are valid places to advertise, but they are established venues. They are also where a lot of your competitors are, which makes it incredibly difficult to compete for attention. Today's communications planners exploit media receptivity tactics to help their clients stand out.

FIVE RECEPTIVITY TACTICS

Five tactics in receptivity planning have proved to be effective uses of media. They are effective because they add to the messaging and branding impact of the communication. The case studies that follow illustrate how the planners developed the following tactics:

- Contextual planning
- Situational advertising
- Leveraging of target passion points
- Branding inside content
- Tapping into consumers' relationship with media

CONTEXTUAL PLANNING

The former Carat chief executive officer David Verklin used to speak of the "moment of aperture," or the moment when consumers are in the right mind-set to think about the product category. For instance, people without an umbrella on a rainy day are greeted as they leave the train station by umbrella sales guys.

We need to tap into media environments and content that reflect those moments. The media environments should be chosen on the basis of a receptivity insight about targeted consumers and how they may interact with that media.

Contextual advertising requires the advertiser to offer a message in a place that works. For example, consider the Hispanic market. The Hispanic population is growing ten times as fast as the general market. Of that population, 73 percent speak Spanish at home. One comment in a focus group that really brought it home to me was "When I see an ad in Spanish, I feel those brands are talking to me."[2] Ads in the right context will always cause more receptivity.

One case that superbly illustrates how a receptivity insight translated to a contextual planning approach is the campaign Optimedia did for Ambien CR.

CASE STUDY: ADVERTISING AT
THE POINT OF NEED: AMBIEN CR

Sanofi-Aventis, the maker of sleep-aid Ambien, was facing new competition as its brand was going generic. The company needed a marketing plan to launch its new formulation, Ambien CR, a controlled-release sleep-aid. It promised "A good night's sleep from start to finish." Its lead competitor, Sepracor's Lunesta, was planning to spend some two hundred million dollars on a media marketing blitz, more than double Ambien CR's annual budget.

As Ambien CR's media agency, we undertook insight work to develop the Brand Media Strategy. For the advertising to resonate, it needed to work at both a creative and a media environment level.

Agency research uncovered two insights about people who suffer from insomnia. The first was an emotional one: sufferers know they don't get enough sleep, but they tend to tough it out. It is not until they are suffering from stress that they become more receptive to messaging from products like Ambien CR. That insight was important as it helped lead to another contextual revelation.

The agency asked, "What kind of relationship do insomniacs have with various media when they are under stress?" The answer was striking. Insomnia sufferers have a very different relationship with all kinds of media when they are under stress. They actively seek out media to help keep them occupied and calm them down. They watch late-night and early-morning television more than nonsufferers. They are more likely to be up watching television or surfing the web on Sunday nights, before the start of the workweek. They are more likely to be visiting travel websites, looking for a getaway. Sufferers tend to watch television to relax and use the web to keep occupied.

We reasoned that if we could tap into media at the moments of stress, consumers would be more receptive to the advertising messages. This simple question about context gave us plenty of clues about when to advertise, where to advertise and how to advertise. Ambien CR combined television and online in a complementary way; television built awareness of the benefit and online gave the detailed explanation of how it worked and distributed a coupon special offer.

Late night and early morning became important times to advertise, in particular Sunday night and Monday morning. Sufferers were most likely thinking about their upcoming working week, a moment of stress. We ran a heavy concentration of Ambien CR commercials during the "morning papers" segment in CNN's now-defunct show *News Night with Aaron Brown*.

The media plan also called for targeting business travelers who experience time-zone changes.

On daylight saving weekend, when the clocks shift forward an hour, people lose an hour of sleep, and the media gives extra attention to insomnia. Ambien CR sponsored a CBS "Healthwatch" feature about time changes and sleep awareness.

Without focusing on media context, it would have been very easy to do just a demographic analysis of insomnia sufferers and run media based on where those demographic audiences could be reached. Ambien CR would have missed a huge opportunity to send highly targeted messages when and where their potential buyers were most engaged with the specific media being used.

In the end, we came up with a plan for Ambien CR that met its volume objectives and cost half of what its new competitor spent. This campaign's receptivity strategy allowed it to cut through.

SITUATIONAL ADVERTISING (BASED ON TACTICAL TIMING)

Situational advertising leverages the right occasion or the right time period for a message to connect most effectively. Similar to contextual planning, situational advertising taps into the consumer's mind-set to increase the receptivity of the messaging. However, in this case, the timing of the messaging is particularly tactical. Running advertising at certain times of day on different media allows the planner to maximize receptivity.

Citroen C5 in the United Kingdom wanted to increase brand consideration among fleet users. Analysis showed that these people had little free time and that they spent most of their work and leisure time in the car.

The planning team used IPA TouchPoints, a database of the mood of consumers across media and time of day. They were able to determine the times of day that drivers would be most alert for running ads about product and functionality. The same research showed that drivers were most relaxed later in the evening. The team ran emotional brand-led ads on television to capitalize on that mind-set.[3]

What about Online Receptivity?

The UK-based Internet Advertising Bureau set out to discover when users were most receptive to ad messaging online. The study found that early evening was the best time of day for all age groups and that younger audiences paid more attention as the day progressed. Older age groups peaked between 9:00 A.M. and 12:00 P.M. and between 2:00 P.M. and 6:00 P.M.[4] The respondents said the best time to reach them with messages was during ecommerce activity, such as researching the best deals or shopping online.

Capturing Occasions and Events to Enhance Receptivity

IKEA stores in the Washington, D.C., area developed a colorful campaign that captured imaginations on a historic occasion. See the case study on page 136, "Furnishing the White House."

LEVERAGING OF TARGET PASSION POINTS

Advertisers can connect to consumers by relating to their passions and interests. Sometimes those passion points are directly related to the brand, sometimes not. Advertisers might create an identity for a brand by association with certain lifestyle activities. Citizen Watches, for instance, espouses tradition and precision and has thus associated itself with the US Open tennis championship for many years.

Another alternative for advertisers is to attach ads to content the consumer is passionate about and create a relationship around that special interest. The US Army used Microsoft's Xbox video game Halo 3 to increase brand consideration by creating a brand experience that expanded on current perceptions of a soldier to reflect an aspirational branch of the military. The ads were aimed at reinforcing the army as a high-tech and cutting-edge profession and extolling the experience, the teamwork and the training.

This is a great example of an advertiser targeting potential recruits through their passions, the largest of which is gaming. The campaign shifted attitudes and perceptions about the service, with 43 percent of gamers recalling the Army sponsorship and leaving with a more positive opinion of the Army.[5]

CASE STUDY: IKEA—FURNISHING THE WHITE HOUSE

The furniture retailer IKEA created an ambitious out-of-home ad campaign that focused on a certain high-profile presidential family that had just moved from Chicago to Washington, D.C. They played up the theme of Barack Obama and his family having to furnish their new home in the White House.

They built a display of the White House's Oval Office fitted with IKEA furniture at Union Station, Washington, D.C.'s main train hub. The display was intended to drive customers to two nearby IKEA stores in College Park, Maryland, and Woodbridge, Virginia. The integrated campaign included billboards carrying the IKEA "Embrace Change '09" slogan on local buses and trains and encouraging home owners to change their furniture. IKEA created a mock motorcade, including the presidential limo, that featured IKEA furniture tied on the vehicles' roofs and was prominently driven around the area.

The www.embracechange09.com website included a place where customers could design their own Oval Office with a drag-and-drop tool and a fifteen-hundred-dollar gift card giveaway to a lucky visitor who visited the site.

The campaign received national attention from the country's media, starved for stories around the inauguration. IKEA public relations director Marty Marston said that IKEA had seized a good branding opportunity: "[Obama's] notion of change and his commitment to fiscal responsibility match the Ikea philosophy of affordable home furnishings for all."[6]

Similarly, our client Toyota's Scion has a brand proposition that promotes being a leading cultural lifestyle brand for Generation Y. The Brand Media Strategy is to influence the influencers and target the opinion formers who can drive brand credibility through their networks and communities. Their approach is to let other brands make a sell through traditional mainstream media, while Scion establishes credibility with their influencers through passionate media venues.

Rather than simply advertise, we use media to build content that entertains and immerses those influencers. The experience has to be authentic and interesting. Our strategy is to make the brand part of the content experience.

We found those opinion formers online at passion sites that helped influence the wider pop culture world. Those sites during this campaign included two music-themed destinations, www.metalinsider.com and www.dubstep.com (a dance music site), and a video game site, gamespy.com. We steered clear of buying anything on Yahoo! or E! or even on MTV.com. The campaign engaged thirty thousand cultural opinion formers in various art forms: film, digital design and music. The campaign reached a further twenty-five million people who visited, interacted and clicked through to the custom-branded content on special-interest publisher sites.

To promote its flat-panel televisions, consumer electronics manufacturer LG used Condé Nast Media Group magazines to tap into their target's passion for film and cinematography. One installment featured film director Edward Zwick (*Glory, The Last Samurai*) in a four-page insert in *Architectural Digest, Vanity Fair, Vogue* and *GQ*. The customized feature showed Zwick on a desert movie set looking at an LG flat-panel television and included his thoughts on cinematography and landscapes. The online portion contained dedicated LG websites on Condé Nast properties, including style.com, concierge.com and wired.com, that featured video interviews with Zwick as well as a behind-the-scenes tour of his Santa Monica, California, office. The focus on Zwick and his experience, not the LG equipment, creates a more emotional link to the LG brand. LG's partnership was noteworthy in that it made Condé Nast both the creator and sole distributor of the ad—a great example of a publisher going beyond just selling traditional media space.

BRANDING INSIDE CONTENT

Product and Brand Placement

Product and brand placement is an effective way of generating increased receptivity. Product placement, product integration and program sponsorship, all under the umbrella term *branded entertainment,* have become much more prominent and much more tactical, particularly in the United States. That growth in use has been fueled by a couple of important developments in the industry. One is the motivation by broadcasters and content providers to defray or subsidize production costs amid more fragmented audiences. Another is the growth of DVRs, now in 35 percent of US households with televisions, which has caused media buyers and sellers to develop "TiVobuster" tactics. Product placement is now opening up in Europe, which in the past largely restricted the appearance of commercial messaging in television programming.

Put simply, branded entertainment works. Sony product placements were all over the 2006 remake of the James Bond movie *Casino Royale.* All characters used Sony VAIO laptops, and a Blu-ray disc is prominent at one point. The characters use Sony Ericsson cell phones, Sony GPS devices and Sony Bravia television sets. Bond uses a Cybershot camera to take photos. Product placement in movies is big business. In *Iron Man,* the main character's alter ego, Tony Stark, scarfs a Burger King cheeseburger. George Clooney flies American Airlines in *Up in the Air.*

Apple Inc. in the week before launching its iPad orchestrated an entire episode of ABC's *Modern Family* consisting of Claire and Phil Dunphy's plight of trying to buy the iPad on the first day it goes on sale. A viewer can spot placements on television any night of the week. None of these appearances happen by chance. They are carefully placed by advertisers and producers as part of commercial ad buys or production sponsorships as ways to engage a receptive audience already locked into a show.

Some pundits cry foul, suggesting that advertisers are crossing the line. There are some egregious examples—some think NBC's *The Restaurant* crossed the line with its close-ups of American Express cards, making advertiser participation a little too obvious. On the whole, advertisers, agencies and program makers want the brand to appear in content in a way that is positive and tasteful. My experience in working with television executives is that viewers themselves provide strong checks and balances that prevent marketers from going too far. If you do something that viewers react to negatively, you'll see a post online or a blog almost immediately. No brand manager or media buyer wants to be responsible for negative feedback.

Product placement is becoming ever more sophisticated. With tongue in cheek, Tina Fey parodies the entire business in an episode of NBC's *30 Rock*. Here's the scene: "Are you all right?" Liz [Lemon, played by Tina Fey] asks boss Jack [Donaghy, played by Alec Baldwin]. "Never mind," Jack replies, glancing at his phone and heading for the door. "These Verizon Wireless phones are just so popular, I accidentally grabbed one belonging to an acquaintance." "Well, sure," Liz replies. "'Cause that Verizon Wireless service is just unbeatable! If I saw a phone like that on TV, I'd be like, 'Where is my nearest retailer so I can get one—?'" Fey stares at the camera with a tight grin. "Can we have our money now?"[7]

This practice of product placement has quickly shifted online. Advertisers are partnering with the digital studio units of big networks or their marketing departments to have them create short-form online content. One example is Sprint, which worked with *Desperate Housewives* creator Marc Cherry to market the show and insert itself into a new online soap opera of mini-episodes penned by Cherry. The writer says he took his inspiration from Taster's Choice commercials, which were formed like mini–soap series.[8]

TAPPING INTO CONSUMERS' RELATIONSHIP WITH MEDIA

Americans spend on average nine hours a day with media. It's become a enormous part of their lives and hugely influences social and cultural fashion. Observing how media is consumed helps us be smarter about how to give messaging real impact. That's the theme of our final receptivity tactic: increasing the relevance of the brand by tapping into the crossroads of media and culture to deliver highly relevant brand communications.

The first case study that follows is one of my personal favorite campaigns. It's about how British phone company Orange advertises at the movies. It's a campaign about gaining acceptance from consumers and about how an advertiser can be welcomed on some occasions by making a positive contribution to the media experience.

The second case revolves around how Toyota tapped into insights of how YouTube was being used and exploited this insight wonderfully for Corolla.

CASE STUDY: ORANGE CINEMA PROMOTION[9]

Phone company Orange created a cinema campaign that one newspaper reviewer described as being better than the movies that followed.[10]

Mother, the agency that conceived the campaign, discovered as much as possible about cinema culture by talking to the audience first as moviegoers, not as consumers of mobile services. The agency came up with a few interesting findings: Since moviegoers had paid to be entertained, they expected to be rewarded by the entire experience, including the ads and the trailers. Because they had this mind-set, they felt that deliberate brand and product placement in movies ruined their experience and was embarrassing to brands. Inside the cinema, mobile phones were unwelcome. If someone else's phone went off, it was annoying, and if you were that someone else, it was mortifying.

To demonstrate self-awareness—that Orange understood all these things—the company created a fictitious Board of Orange, which had company executives sit behind a desk adjudicating marketing pitches and movie ideas in a comedic series featuring film directors and actors including the likes of Spike Lee, Carrie Fisher, Ewan McGregor and Sigourney Weaver. Their characters personified all the ruinous influences that brands and marketing have had on the cinema experience.

While it was a risky marketing effort, it showed cultural intelligence. The dialogue was laced with movie references to show how deeply Orange was involved in movie culture. They made the obligatory "turn off your phone" message more entertaining. They created Orange Wednesdays, when Orange customers could take a friend to the cinema for free.

The results proved that the Orange cinema spots delivered significant brand recognition and talkability. Of all the communications channels that Orange invests in, cinema continues to have the most positive impact on the brand.

CASE STUDY: TOYOTA LAUGHS IT UP WITH YOUTUBE[11]

For the launch of the 2008 model Corolla, Toyota was trying to reach young adults in their late teens and early twenties. Marketers know that this group is hard to reach at the best of times, and the emergence of digital media has made this job is even tougher.

As one of America's top-spending brands on television, Toyota knows that television viewing by this demographic group has been falling in recent years. One solution has been to shift more money for youth-oriented products to online advertising and events. Yet the problem with advertising strategies that "push" the message over to the web is the tremendous number of sites available to youth. The audience is highly fragmented and many sites don't lend themselves to the kind of relevant, noninterruptive messaging that a younger audience values.

Toyota and its agency, Saatchi & Saatchi LA, solved this problem with a combination of consumer insight, contextual insight and good old-fashioned media planning basics. The first insight was clear: to reach a young audience, a brand needed to be on the web. Whether web or television, Toyota needed to find a broad-reach channel.

On the web, few sites offer the kind of reach necessary to fulfill that goal. While Facebook and YouTube were sites that might work, they were not the kind of sites that could accommodate interruptive advertising. The key was to find a way to work with such broad-reach sites to enhance the user experience instead of detracting from it. This was particularly important for Corolla, a car with a boring heritage, but one that now offered a model perfectly styled and priced for young people. That's where the contextual insights came in.

Saatchi & Saatchi LA's executive communications director, John Lisko, set his team to the task. They quickly came up with a simple, powerful contextual insight: the content people seek out on YouTube is very different from television. On YouTube they were looking at predominantly short and funny films. With this thought in mind, the team realized that they could do a lot more than just push a digital advertisement on YouTube. They could use the site as a medium to pull in consumers, offering young viewers a chance to see the best-of-the-best of funny short clips and a chance get involved in the comedy content that they loved. Out of this insight, two YouTube–Toyota Corolla initiatives were born: "Best in Jest" and "Sketchies," both powered by YouTube and custom designed for Toyota

"Best in Jest," launched in March of 2008, is a repository for the funniest videos of the week. It is sponsored by Corolla and features funny videos of the Corolla brand for those who wish to view them. The "Best in Jest" collection adds value to the YouTube experience, allowing people to see the funniest videos quickly without having to find them via countless hours of searching.

"Sketchies" is a site where the viewing community can submit short comedy sketch videos to be judged for cash and prizes. The videos had to include a road trip (for obvious reasons) and a musical instrument (just for fun). "Best in Jest" and "Sketchies" allowed Corolla to be relevant as an advertiser on YouTube because they understood the context and made the most of it for YouTube users.

The results were outstanding. Saatchi & Saatchi LA reported that the campaign resulted in a significant increase in brand favorability and purchase consideration among respondents who had visited the sites. One of the most impressive statistics was the result that 55 percent of visitors to the "Sketchies" contest said they would consider purchasing a Corolla.

Saatchi's Lisko attributes the success to the power of the original media insight: "This campaign was the difference between advertising on YouTube and creating a new YouTube experience that was relevant to a young audience and a perfect fit for Corolla. Corolla was adding value, not taking away. Working with new media is about understanding three things: context, context, and context. When media insights get a seat at the creative table amazing things can happen."

Exploiting media context and media environments can amplify the creative messaging to deliver more relevant and involved brand communications. Uncovering moments of receptivity is a key tactic for driving engagement. These five receptivity tactics have proved to be a powerful means of delivering highly effective brand media strategies.

QUESTIONS TO ASK TO FIND WAYS TO EXPLOIT RECEPTIVITY IN MEDIA

1. What insights do we have of how audiences are using individual media vehicles or touch points and what do they tell us about how to communicate better to them?

2. Put yourself in the target consumer's shoes. What factors would make the messaging more relevant or interesting to him or her?

3. If you're in the market for a product, in which media would you actively look for information and ideas about the product category?

4. In what places, occasions or times would the consumer most likely be more open to finding out more about this product category?

5. What places would be less appropriate to advertise in terms of receptivity?

CHAPTER 9

TOUCH POINT SELECTION

DETERMINING THE RIGHT
MEDIA CHANNEL MIX

THINK LIKE AN INVESTMENT FUND MANAGER

Communications planners are, in effect, investment managers. We manage large sums of money. We advise our clients where to invest. We analyze which media are going to give better returns. And we recommend a strategy of how best to do it. In the case of an advertiser, those returns are defined by the communication goals.

Fund managers first determine which broad sectors to invest in. They look at the fundamentals, the macro factors—which areas show potential, which are less risky and which to discount. Then there is stock picking, our equivalent of media planning. Media planners take the budget and determine the best options to buy.

An investment manager once told me that 65 percent of an investment portfolio's returns are determined by going into the right sectors and markets. The balance of the return comes from stock picking. Media works the same way.

INVESTING IN THE RIGHT TOUCH POINTS

An important element of the Brand Media Strategy is integrating the brand communications across the different touch points in a way that best exploits the target consumer's relationship with each of the channels. As we'll see later in this chapter, Italian pasta maker Buitoni saw better results from its marketing by using touch points that stimulated a last-minute buy at the supermarket. For the delivery company UPS, in explaining its offering, video presented the most effective tool.

The job of the communications planner is to first consider *all* possible touch points. Next we refine the selection of these touch points by deciding which will achieve maximum synergy with the message.

It is through this process that we determine the combination of media exposure and consumer experiences. Creating the best marketing integration comes from embracing true media neutrality, evaluating the metrics of each channel and then activating tactics that deliver the communication goals. This is a blend of science and art. But it's also driven by a need to make the right choices and trade-offs to ensure the Brand Media Strategy is focused and sells.

This chapter will explain how to identify the core touch points and determine how they work together.

IN MARKETING, WE'RE ALL CHANNEL BIASED

Every executive has his or her own bias about which media works best—from the creative director who's sold award-winning television campaigns his entire career to the digital-savvy account planner who favors social media solutions over traditional media campaigns. Big media agencies are sometimes accused of favoring mass media over niche ones. The digital agency will always be pitching for a bigger share of the budget, and so on.

Clients are the same. Procter & Gamble continues to spend the vast majority of its budget on television advertising. Some clients, in contrast, show a distinct bias against traditional media, challenging the agency to explore the next bright and shiny thing. The onus on the communications planner is to be the umpire.

THE IMPORTANCE OF BEING MEDIA NEUTRAL

Being media neutral shifts the thinking from share of voice to share of mind. Everything can be a medium. Every medium can project the brand, from a television ad to direct mail, from a conversation with a sales assistant to the product's packaging.

Owned media is media that incorporates a company's own content, packaging, point of sale and people who come into contact with consumers. This includes the trucks that transport the product and the product demonstrators inside supermarkets. *Earned media* is PR, buzz, recommendation and advice prompted by influencers and consumers.

Paid, earned and owned media all contribute to brand and purchase influence. Each media form works differently, which needs to be taken into consideration when planning how to use them. Figure 9.1 describes each of the three media.

RIGHT MEDIA FOR THE RIGHT JOB

Different media create different experiences, and some are better suited to certain communication goals. A study evaluated which were the key mass media on the basis of how budgets were allocated by primary marketing objectives.[1] It found what we instinctively know to be true. Television is more suited to the brand objective of creating awareness. Magazines are better for promoting consideration. Newspapers and the internet are more used in driving traffic or purchase intent (see figure 9.2).

FIGURE 9.1

Definition of Owned, Paid and Earned Media

Media Type	Definition	Examples	The Role	Benefits	Challenges
Owned media	Channel a brand controls	• Website • Mobile site • Blog • Twitter account	Build for longer-term relationships with existing potential customers and earn media	• Control • Cost efficiency • Longevity • Versatility • Niche audiences	• No guarantees • Company communication not trusted • Takes time to scale
Paid media	Brand pays to leverage a channel	• Display ads • Paid search • Sponsorships	Shift from foundation to a catalyst that feeds owned and creates earned media	• In demand • Immediacy • Scale • Control	• Clutter • Declining response rates • Poor credibility
Earned media	When customers become the channel	• WOM • Buzz • Viral	Listen and respond — earned media is often the result of well-executed owned and paid media	• Most credible • Key role in most sales • Transparent and lives on	• No control • Can be negative • Scale • Hard to measure

Source: Forrester Research, "No Media Should Stand Alone," December 16, 2009.

FIGURE 9.2

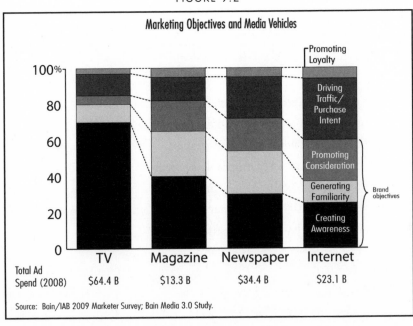

Source: Bain/IAB 2009 Marketer Survey; Bain Media 3.0 Study.

CASE STUDY: PICKWICK AFTERNOON SPIRIT— ANALYZING THE MEDIA MIX

Sara Lee International developed a campaign for their tea brand Pickwick. A new variant, Pickwick Afternoon Spirit, was an herbal blend based on natural ingredients (including peppermint, chamomile and licorice), which was launched over a fifteen-week campaign in the Netherlands between December 2004 and April 2005. The three chief objectives for the advertising campaign were to increase unaided product awareness, proposition awareness and purchase intent.

The media mix for this campaign consisted of television (43%), print with sampling (48%) and online (8%). Daphne Communication Management executed cross-media research via a weekly online questionnaire measuring the impact of this campaign against the identified metrics.

It's rare to see such well-defined forensics of a media mix. So I've included the findings to give the reader more awareness of how each medium influenced the effectiveness of the overall campaign.

The campaign was a success, as illustrated by the campaign results: Product awareness increased 36 percent. Purchase intent increased 35 percent. Proposition awareness increased 20 percent.[2]

TELEVISION

Television was effective at generating awareness about the new product introduction. The largest build-up of awareness was achieved during the first television flight. It, however, did not communicate the product proposition of Pickwick Afternoon Spirit.

PRINT

The print campaign on its own was not as effective as the other media at driving any of the campaign metrics. This was largely attributed to the creative execution. However, in the case of consumers who were exposed to either the television or online and print, awareness and purchase intent increased significantly. Thanks to samples, print achieved product trial but a high level of frequency was needed.

ONLINE

Online was by far the most cost-effective medium. It made an especially large contribution on cognitive elements such as brand knowledge. It also played well in tandem with print and television. Daphne concluded that spreading the internet campaign over many weeks to reach a larger audience with a low contact frequency helped the brand.

CONCLUSIONS AND INSIGHTS

Awareness of brand and proposition of Pickwick Afternoon Spirit rose significantly thanks to a positive transfer of message in television commercials and online. At the start of the campaign there was a less obvious transfer of message in print advertisements. However, there was a large increase of buying intention and buying behavior during the campaign.

OVERALL LEARNING

Different media offered different benefits: Television drove awareness and brand metrics. Magazines prompted response and action. Online drove brand familiarity. The combined media mix drove brand measures. Creativity in each medium is still a strong factor in value of communication. The impact of frequency is harder to judge and is different by media.

TOUCH POINT SELECTION CRITERIA

A number of tools are available to steer and measure the decision making. But selecting touch points requires making judgments to anticipate how individual campaigns need to be communicated. We must constantly evaluate how the selected touch points leverage the campaign's creative messaging and the use of media.

At this part of the planning stage, putting the money in the right buckets is more important than execution. This stage takes a first pass at effectiveness evaluation and determining the broad tactical use of media. Once these are known, then the specifics of how to implement each medium are developed. So, for example, step one is to select television, determine the budget and set the primary television goals. In step two, the planner and broadcast team determine which stations, time periods and activation tactics will be employed to meet the goals and to maximize efficiency.

THREE INPUTS BEHIND TOUCH POINT SELECTION

Three inputs determine the selection process: data, consumer insight and communication needs (figure 9.3). These three inputs provide complementary or contradictory forces in making selection decisions. For example, response data may prove that search is a more targeted medium for delivering acquisitions, but if there is a brand problem with consideration, television might be a better choice.

Touch point selection calls for making trade-offs based on what the campaign needs to do and therefore what is more important. Each campaign is going to be a balance of these three factors.

DATA-LED DECISION MAKING

Investment decisions need to be supported by good data. Many clients want to see analytic rigor and fact-based recommendations. The communications planning world draws on three main sources: market-mix (or econometric)

FIGURE 9.3

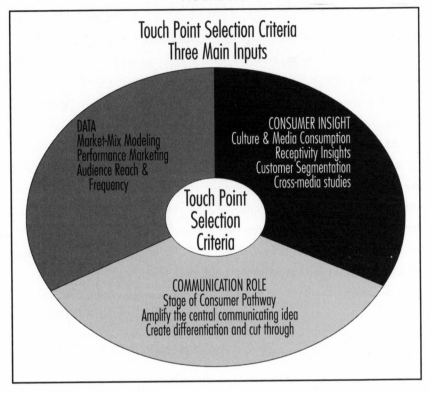

Touch Point Selection Criteria
Three Main Inputs

DATA
Market-Mix Modeling
Performance Marketing
Audience Reach &
Frequency

CONSUMER INSIGHT
Culture & Media Consumption
Receptivity Insights
Customer Segmentation
Cross-media studies

Touch Point
Selection
Criteria

COMMUNICATION ROLE
Stage of Consumer Pathway
Amplify the central communicating idea
Create differentiation and cut through

modeling, performance marketing and media audience–based data. The different levels and degrees of robustness of the data, as well as stability of variables in future planned marketing, dictate the level of confidence in these sources.

MARKET-MIX MODELING

Market-mix, or econometric, modeling has been used by marketers since the seventies. It's the gold standard, particularly for high-spending, regular-purchase products. Market-mix modeling gives specific measurement on which media delivers better return on investment (ROI) to sales. It helps determine and fine-tune the channel or media mix. The communications planner uses modeling to shift dollars toward the more efficient media and places that deliver higher ROI. The approach tends to work best when marketers' conditions are stable and there is consistent spending that provides lots of data points.

PERFORMANCE MARKETING

Data-based planning helps determine the consumer's response to advertising. This is most obvious in direct response campaigns that prompt consumers to visit a site or dial a number. Performance marketing provides very specific data such as click-through rates or the level of audience interaction.

Performance metrics are rapidly becoming the most significant media currency. Capturing behavior gives a richer understanding of the engagement and value to an advertiser. It also provides more real-time data for targeting, testing, adjusting and improving the response of the media plan. This responsiveness has greatly increased media's ability to deliver greater accountability.

Performance marketing is most significant in digital and direct response media, but it will fast move into other media forms. For example, mobile media such as Apple's iPads, interactive television and social media platforms are used as direct response media.

REACH AND FREQUENCY

Reach and frequency remain standard measures of a media outlet's breadth of impact. *Reach* measures the coverage that each channel delivers; *frequency* is how often a person is exposed to an advertising message. They continue to be universal means to gauge the delivery of the message and therefore potential influence on awareness, involvement and consideration goals.

EFFECTIVENESS, EFFICIENCY, SCALE

Optimedia's head of analytics, Rudy Grahn, describes what planners need to consider in selecting touch points: "You need to be evaluating effectiveness, efficiency and scale."[3]

Effectiveness refers to judging the media's ability to influence the consumer or create a response. So the emphasis is on the level of exposure, engagement of the impressions or, in the case of online, the click-through rate or cost of sales. Different research techniques have their own ways to define effectiveness, but usually an almost limitless number of different methodologies and currencies quantify a medium's potential engagement or quality of exposure. We elaborate on this further in chapter 12, "Measurement and Metrics."

Efficiency refers to the relative cost effectiveness of the media: the cost per thousand (CPM) impressions, cost per click or cost per sale. Efficiency is fairly simple to measure once effectiveness is quantified.

Scale, the third factor, refers to the overall communication or marketing goals. If a company wants to sell one million units, then the most cost-effective or efficient medium may not be sufficient. To break that point down a little further: Online may be the most cost-efficient medium to acquire customers. Creating awareness through television may not be as efficient and may require significant initial ad-production costs and be less measurable. However, television may ensure achieving critical mass in the product trial and take-up. That's one big reason why major advertisers aren't putting 100 percent of their budget into online even if the data suggests this is more cost effective. Advertisers need a combination of media to achieve their goals.

CONSUMER-INSIGHT-LED TOUCH POINT SELECTION

Chapter 7 discusses the central communicating idea, developed from consumer insight and guiding touch point selection and use.

Receptivity is also an important input in determining touch point selection. Chapter 8 showed how we could select media by exploiting receptivity of the messaging through use of context-based insights.

A third area of insight comes from employing cross-media studies.

CROSS-MEDIA STUDIES

Surveys such as MRI and Simmonds in the United States; or TGI, which operates in sixty-seven countries internationally; or EGM in Latin American countries are syndicated single-source research databases that combine media consumption with product and brand usage and consumer attitudes. They allow some cross-media comparisons to use in touch point selection. Development of different research techniques provides better science to support the judgment of the communications planner. Here is a selection of some of the more progressive tools.

IPA TOUCHPOINTS INITIATIVE

The IPA TouchPoints Initiative was created and designed for UK communications agencies. I sat on the IPA Media Futures Group that sponsored this industry-wide initiative, but much of the credit goes to Lynne Robinson, research director at the IPA, for spearheading this study.

Its primary objective is to give communication strategists insight into how people are using the increasingly wide range of media available to them and how this usage fits into their lifestyles. IPA TouchPoints was designed as a stand-alone survey that allows integration of other media research currencies and surveys. It measures all media usage, including television, print, radio, internet, social networking, search and mobile phone usage. It also looks at retail activity, what people are doing and their mood. For example, sports betting company Coral used the database to determine that readers of the *Mail on Sunday* read the paper while also watching sports on television. Thus Coral knew this combination of media would be extremely relevant and consumers highly receptive to its advertising message.

The study provides cross-media data to help intermedia decision making. It collects the data on PDAs, allowing live reporting of consumer habits rather than the inconsistent diary method. This very successful format is being adopted in several other countries, including a planned rollout in the United States.

MEDIADNA

MediaDNA is a system developed initially in the United Kingdom and was conceived by Frank Harrison, global head of strategic resources at Zenith-

Optimedia. It later became an industry-wide tool. The system selects media brands according to their brand personality. A planner could select a magazine or a television show on the basis of whether it was perceived as innovative or intelligent. Defining brand personalities enables media and brand matchmaking for brands that want to use media vehicles to develop or reinforce certain brand qualities. For instance, *Cosmopolitan* might be seen by readers as "confident" or "brash," qualities that might pair well with a cosmetics brand hoping to own those same attributes.

SELECTING TOUCH POINTS BASED ON COMMUNICATIONS ROLE

THE CONSUMER PATHWAY

The main questions to ask when determining the communications role are: What stage of the Consumer Pathway are we trying to target? How will we amplify the central communicating idea? And how will this create differentiation?

Figure 9.4 gives a visual estimation of different media and their relative impact at different stages of the Consumer Pathway. I say estimation because these are only generalizations based on common use. This estimation helps determine the different role each touch point needs to play in the overall campaign. Going back to Pickwick Afternoon Spirit, television's role was to generate awareness. Online's was to drive knowledge that would aid consideration. Magazine's role was to deliver trial and use. Each medium needs to have a specific and defined role to play in the overall communications plan.

The Buitoni case illustrates our touch-point strategy of selecting media by clearly defining their communication roles. It shows how we combined consumer insight with the communication goal to formulate a touch-point strategy. We first had to increase involvement by amplifying the creative idea through a very specific media selection, and then we drove active consideration by tapping into touch points that influenced the shopper close to the time of purchase.

FIGURE 9.4

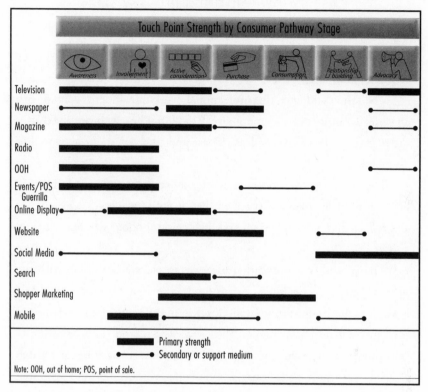

CREATING DIFFERENTIATION AND CUT-THROUGH

The Brand Media Strategy must take into account the competitive context.

If every car company advertises in the same car magazines, on the same websites and in the same Super Bowl, because "that's where car drivers are," their ads won't be effective. The Brand Media Strategy should look different from its rivals. And that's why, for communications planning, exceptions are often the rule. So while there are established places and best-practice uses of media (for example, television for awareness, newspapers for retail, online for information), a planner needs to balance that with thinking outside the box in order to break through.

A great example, and one of my favorite media campaigns, was the long-running outdoor advertising campaign of the *Economist*. The billboard ads,

CASE STUDY: BUITONI CHILLED PASTA— A RECIPE FOR TOUCH POINT SELECTION

Nestlé's Buitoni chilled pasta product had the marketing challenge of reviving sagging sales.

The target audience was professional, working, affluent women with an annual household income above $75,000. The customer lived in a metro city on the West or East Coast and likely lived in a two-adult household.

The company wanted to market its chilled pasta as a premium product, but its media plan didn't reflect that. Buitoni needed to *act* premium and reflect that in their speech and the decisions about where ads would appear.

The central communicating idea was to elevate the brand with the phrase "Buitoni: The Italian art of food." Previous campaigns had followed category conventions too closely—meaning they chose women's food magazines. The television they were using, food shows and shows targeting women, wasn't forcing brand reappraisal. The campaign needed to recognize the target's busy working lifestyle and specific shopping habits and let those be the key criteria for determining the touch-point selection. While food environments remained relevant, they could not be relied on to change behavior. The brand had to get beyond traditional ideas of where pasta advertising belongs in determining the change.

The product had low household penetration, and the client stated that the main aim was to stimulate trial. Past media campaigns had centered on maximizing awareness and reach. However, given that chilled pasta is an unplanned just-in-time purchase and that the target shops two to three times per week, our communications planner argued for more frequency. Instead of setting the standard frequency goal of three or more times (that is, hitting consumers with advertising an optimal three times), the campaign was analyzed on frequency levels of nine or more times. Additionally, given the just-in-time purchase habit, there was a need to be present at the point of purchase.

Daytime online, out-of-home media and in-store touch points all played a much more significant role in the media plan. To amplify the "the Italian art of food" platform, we developed the campaign to look like an art form. The out-of-home element of the campaign featured a subway art gallery: one hundred framed "masterpieces" of Buitoni dishes hung on the walls at New York's Union Square subway. Buitoni handed out gallery guides at the station and made audio tours available on cell phones. The combination of touch points closer to purchase and amplifying the creative idea was responsible for increasing sales immediately. Product purchase grew 19 percent in the advertised markets.

with simple white type on a red background resembling the *Economist*'s masthead, contained humorous headlines, such as "I don't read the *Economist*—management trainee, aged 42."

When promoting a magazine to business readers, the data would have sent the *Economist* to advertise in the obvious spaces, for example, other business magazines, financial pages of newspapers, possibly in airports, in-flight areas and hotels—exactly where the *Economist*'s competitors advertised. The *Economist* opted instead for a broad outdoor campaign that stood out and delivered the message creatively and with absolute consistency. The differentiation of their strategies made sure there was clear space and distinctiveness in their media campaigns. This campaign consistently delivered increased subscription growth for the *Economist*.

INFLUENCE AND CLUTTER

One analysis I like to use to help steer touch-point selection is the influence-clutter analysis. Plotting media on a grid ranking influence (which could be reach, engagement, audience appeal or whatever measure a planner decides is important) and clutter (concentration of advertising by category) gives a good opportunity to develop a touch-point selection strategy.

Figure 9.5 shows an influence-clutter analysis for a brand in the auto-motive category. It ranks a medium by its influence, in this case media com-position, or the concentration of the brand's prime target audience each medium draws. It also tracks each medium in terms of level of competitor spending. Media fall into four quadrants (see figure 9.6).

The influence-clutter analysis identifies, selects and determines how to exploit touch points on the basis of what's happening in the category.

In this example, cable television and business publications are influen-tial but heavily used by all the competition. We recommended lifestyle pub-lications to this client, which were as influential as business publications but had the benefit of having few or no competitors in them. This gave the brand plan some clear space to help them stand out.

FIGURE 9.5

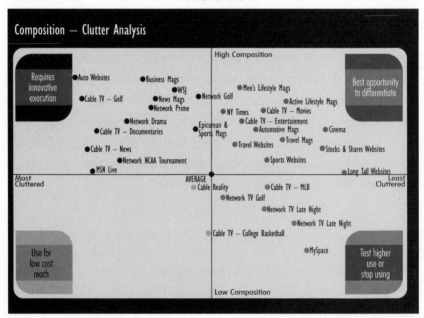

FIGURE 9.6

Influence — Clutter Quadrants		
Influence	Category Clutter	Potential Tactics
High	High	Need to probably use, but it is important to differentiate
High	Low	Look to exploit, opportunity to differentiate
Low	High	Avoid or use to deliver efficient reach and frequency
Low	Low	Try to test or avoid

OTHER FACTORS A PLANNER NEEDS TO CONSIDER

CREATIVE INPUT

Touch-point selection should be initially led by the communications planners, but as with most things in the communications process, the final plan is a collaborative effort. Importantly, the initial recommendation draws from data and insights into how the media channels interact and reach their audiences. Then the Brand Media Strategy is fine-tuned and developed by the communications planner alongside the creative and account planners.

USE OF NONTRADITIONAL MEDIA

Much of our discussion on touch points has centered on mass media or digital media, but they're not the only options. Some brands have ignored media advertising altogether.

A good example of a brand that built itself without the help of traditional media is Red Bull. The energy drink has turned experiential media into an art form. The brand avoided traditional media, instead sponsoring alternative events such as the Red Bull Flugtag, an air show event. I was in Paris recently with other agency colleagues. Red Bull had just been launched in the French market after having been banned from being sold there. A bar's television ran a continuous video of the multiple extreme sports events that Red Bull is involved with. It made for compelling content that kept us glued to the screen. It was an incredibly effective example of owned media playing a strong role at a key distribution venue.

FEWER, BIGGER, BETTER

The growing list of touch points available leads to planners often trying to incorporate just too many touch points within a plan.

Too many media outlets dilute the messaging and impact the budget as production costs increase. Spreading a campaign thinly across media makes it harder to cut through and reduces frequency, which is important for effectiveness. It also reduces leverage with media vendors. My advice is to be more strategic and make an active decision about which media will make the biggest difference.

Selecting touch points is a process that requires the plan to be focused and the planner to make good trade-offs. Touch-point selection should be deliberate, to pinpoint the right ones.

DEFINING THE ROLE OF TOUCH POINTS IN THE COMMUNICATIONS STRATEGY

Once the touch points have been identified, the next stage is to clearly articulate their role. This guides the specialist activation teams in developing better tactical solutions in media.

Different touch points can perform multiple potential roles in the Brand Media Strategy. A medium can perform many tasks. Take television as an example. Television is strongly suited for efficiently and effectively generating awareness of new products or a new brand feature. It can increase brand involvement through sponsorship, build familiarity through product placement or drive more product understanding through advertising spots. Television can increase brand consideration by promoting a competitive claim, sending consumers to a website for more information or boosting foot traffic to a store with a special promotion. Television can also directly sell a product through long-form telemarketing response campaigns. And we all know that if an ad hits the screen during the Super Bowl, it can drive word of mouth or get people to go online. Online, print, radio, out-of-home, mobile and nontraditional media can all play numerous roles for brands. For the Brand Media Strategy to work, the planner needs to specify how to activate each touch point.

The UPS "Whiteboard" campaign demonstrates this point nicely.[4] The creative involves a spokesperson simply writing on a whiteboard. The brand used television to create launch-level brand awareness with high reach and frequency. It was a very visual campaign. They wanted to amplify the whiteboard device, so they featured sportscasters using a whiteboard to explain complicated plays on television, and financial analysts using a whiteboard to analyze the market, and television networks creating animated whiteboard introductions and summaries of programs.

Online video was the strongest platform for the "Whiteboard" idea to demonstrate the brand campaign, and online search was used to drive traffic and customers to their website.

In print, UPS needed to get to core business customers but also to amplify the creative idea. The video component of "Whiteboard" has a strong revelation moment when the solution provided by UPS is unveiled to the consumer. To achieve the same feeling of revelation in print, they took alternate space such as bookend units in the *Wall Street Journal,* flap pages in the small-business magazine *Inc.* and consecutive half-page spreads in *Business Week.*

They selected very targeted, high-reach, out-of-home vehicles designed to surprise their business targets by communicating to them in ways UPS had not in years past. They included train and bus station sites in New York City and three-dimensional billboards on commuter arteries.

The results of the Brand Media Strategy were very positive. Awareness not only grew but also eroded much more slowly than expected once the flight was over, showing the impact of these tactics. Site traffic exceeded UPS's expectations, with thousands of actions taken on the site.

QUESTIONS TO ASK WHEN
MAKING TOUCH POINT SELECTIONS

1. Does the mix have the right balance between reach, engagement and efficiency?
2. Do the recommended touch points amplify the central communicating idea?
3. How do the touch point selections differentiate compared with the competition?
4. Are there clearly defined communication roles for each touch point?

CHAPTER 10

DIGITIZING THE BRAND MEDIA STRATEGY

NOT JUST ANOTHER MEDIUM

I've talked to several media agency chief executive officers who subscribe to the view that digital media is just another medium, and like television or magazines, it should be planned and managed in the same way.

I couldn't disagree more. Digital championed by the likes of Google and Facebook has changed the rules, setting up our new media playbook.

Digital isn't one medium, it is many media, and the list is ever expanding.

A key difference between digital and other media is that innovation is the very essence of the medium. The DNA of digital media companies is that they are in a constant state of reinvention. This is a young industry, and its leaders seem obsessed with breaking convention. If only other media shared that trait.

The evidence for the perpetual state of change of digital media marketing is plain. The internet metamorphosed from essentially a direct response advertising medium of banners, email marketing and search to what it has become today. It is preeminent as an ecommerce platform—think of the ubiquity of Amazon and eBay. It is a social media facilitator on both PC and mobile devices. It threatens to be television's most direct competitor. All this in just fifteen years!

Digital media, as a brand and marketing communications channel, has opened up the stages of the Consumer Pathway that other media weren't as effective at influencing. This has given more dimension and utility to Brand Media Strategies.

WHY SHOULD DIGITAL HAVE ITS OWN CHAPTER?

So if one of the rules of the new media playbook is to be media neutral, why single out digital? Because digital expands brand communications. It brings interactivity and opportunity to personalize communication. But it is a medium still underutilized despite its potential.

Increasingly inventive digital tactics are being employed. This chapter is designed to inspire readers to explore and exploit digital options.

Online will become the second-biggest advertising medium in the world by 2012.[1] Digital's potential is being realized by marketers, but not fully. Needham & Co. media analyst Laura Martin notes, "Audience migration has decoupled from monetization." She points out that people spend 15 percent of their time with the web, which receives only 8 percent of the dollars.[2]

ONLINE CAN INCREASE BRAND MEDIA INFLUENCE

Online's value as a brand medium has taken on more prominence. Communications planners exploit tactics that deliver more engaged communications, fuel brand conversations and target more relevant messages to audiences. We cover these more specifically later in this chapter.

We also explore how digital complements other mass media opportunities, for example, used in tandem with a Super Bowl promotion. We look at how the likes of Facebook, Twitter and YouTube have become extensions to the traditional media solutions. And we also illustrate how online content has become much more than advertising.

THE EARLY CHALLENGES OF DIGITAL INTEGRATION

It has often been a struggle to integrate digital with general advertising. This is in part due to the digital marketing community's origins. Digital agencies grew up as independent specialists outside the mainstream creative shops. Initially, this happened in part because the mainstream agencies were slow to engage digital. The internet in the late 1990s was largely viewed as a direct response medium rather than a branding medium—the lifeblood of ad agencies. It did not help that ad agencies, where creative is king, were largely low-tech organizations.

Entrepreneurs backed with venture capitalist funding seized the initiative from the established ad agencies and jumped into new media. This breed of digital agency was very different from that of your typical ad shop. These agencies were analytic, entrepreneurial, tech savvy and motivated to turn the establishment on its head. This difference was replicated on the client side. Whether client or agency, the division was probably driven by a lack of comfort with digital by the general practitioners. But it was also partly that digital managers wanted to preserve their sovereignty and independence from the nondigital managers. When I ran my own digital agency, I have to admit that I was guilty of digital snobbery, all too ready to claim that the traditional agencies and clients didn't get it. We were online and they were offline. We were new media; they were traditional media.

But of course, the desire of digital executives to get a seat at the top table and infiltrate the bigger brand budgets, along with the financial crisis that began in 2008, brought an end to this separatist culture. The agency holding companies began to acquire digital agencies. The integration and cross-pollination of skills and organizations was a logical move but not without challenges. Some deep-seated cultural differences remain.

AGENCIES DIGITIZING

At Optimedia we embarked on our own digitization program. This involved several steps.

We encouraged the communications planners to learn on the job by taking an active daily interest in this discipline. We asked planners and buyers across all disciplines to subscribe to some of the excellent email newsletters available on the subject. We stepped up digital-training sessions, webinars, lunch-and-learn programs and workshops. We more clearly defined the role of communications planners. We redefined the responsibilities of the senior agency planners and client leads, asking them to take more ownership in digital. We encouraged a more collaborative rather than controlling approach with the digital team. We built digital into our communications planning process and reorganized to integrate working practices between planning, buying and digital. Most importantly, we challenged the senior agency management themselves to upskill in digital. Finally, we celebrated smart integrated work in our internal awards program.

When Publicis Groupe acquired Digitas I was impressed with how determined Digitas chief executive officer David Kenny was to break down the walls and how quickly he inserted Digitas personnel into the rest of the company. VivaKi, the unit that sits atop all Publicis Groupe media and digital agencies, facilitates integration and doubles as a research and development unit charged with fostering digital innovation inside and outside the company.

A DIGITAL MANIFESTO

The vision at our agency was to become an organization that delivered truly integrated media communications solutions. We developed a manifesto for delivering integrated digital strategies for our clients. The manifesto laid out our expectations of the understanding, expertise and responsibilities required and invoked a spirit of partnership between the communications planning and digital teams. We wanted to foster two-way communication, respect for each other's crafts and collaboration.

Below is an extract from that manifesto.

COMMUNICATIONS PLANNER RESPONSIBILITIES

- Should be adept at articulating to clients digital's role and a budget mix rationale within the overall communication plan, and how that will deliver against the business challenge
- Should be familiar [with] and able to explain broadly the key digital strategies of the plan
- Should be aware of the digital strategies taking place in their clients' category
- Should be up-to-date on latest digital metrics and trends, particularly their application to clients' potential media plans, specifically online display, search, online video and social media
- Keep themselves apprised of new and emerging technologies
- Manage integrated communication flow charts and budgets
- Be able to effectively brief and inspire great digital work
- The communications planner and the digital planner should jointly develop the overall digital strategy.

DIGITAL PLANNERS NEED TO:

- Expect strong briefs and return strong work
- Share the digital tactics strategy with communications planners before issuing the RFP to vendors with ample time to be explained and aligned
- Accept the communications planner view of the overall plan and input into the digital plans
- Help update communications planners on digital category innovations
- Keep the communications planning lead well informed (i.e., no surprises) if communicating with the general client
- Review campaign performance with communications planners, but it should be incumbent upon the communications planner to evaluate overall media campaign performance.

We developed and wrote this manifesto a few years ago. It remains as relevant today as it was then.

WHAT SHOULD WE BE DOING ON FACEBOOK?

"How should we be exploiting mobile commerce?" "Are we looking into Four Square yet?" Often clients throw these questions, and the Facebook question, at a planner. When the latest new thing surfaces, companies want to know if they should get on board. Many times, the client's chief executive officer reads an article in the *Wall Street Journal* and fires off an email to his or her marketing team asking, "Are we doing this?"

This happens every day in our business. It's easy to default to digital tactics or individual digital channels. Another trap that agency people fall into is the scattergun approach. Digital people (and I was one of them once upon a time) are prone to believe that digital can solve *all* marketing needs. As a digital planner or account director, it is ingrained that one of your primary roles is to sell the channel. The evangelism goes something like this: "Digital can help you drive response, it can help you to create buzz, it can build awareness, it can help create brand engagement."

When I ran my digital firm, I would meet with a marketing director and tell him we could solve 90 percent of all his marketing problems on the internet—and that was back in 1999! Before Google AdWords and Facebook existed. Before broadband, online video or dynamic mobile internet. For credibility with general marketing clients, digital planners need to ensure they are balanced in their recommendations of channel use.

START WITH THE STRATEGY, NOT THE TACTICS

The best way to respond to eager clients and avoid the scattergun approach is to ask, "What is your Brand Media Strategy?" And then, "What digital media or tactics address your strategy?"

For digital to be integrated and effective it needs to be part of an overall communications strategy. Digital can't do everything, all the time. So not only does communications planning need to integrate digital, but digital needs to be integrated into the Brand Media Strategy.

Develop the Brand Media Strategy first and make digital the first step. The Brand Media Strategy allows the agency team to guide and filter the tactics, but my advice is to prioritize digital options.

DIGITAL AS A SUPPORT MEDIUM

In many cases, the planner or brand manager may decide it makes sense for other media to lead a campaign. For example, television could be the best choice for driving awareness or launching a product or event. In the fashion market, print remains the key influencing medium to drive opinion and trends. In both cases, digital's role becomes support.

The question must therefore be, What can digital add? The brand strategy needs digital to supplement, not duplicate, other media. Remember, the skill of the communications planner is *integration*, not replication.

There's no point in digital trying to build awareness if television can do it more quickly and cost efficiently. Digital may add audiences not reached by the television buy, but sometimes it makes sense to add more stations and ratings on the television plan.

SOCIAL MEDIA AS A BRANDING TOOL

We've discussed the influence Facebook, MySpace, LinkedIn, Twitter and other social media have had in the digital space and branding. There's a lot of experimentation in social media, as few standard advertising models for it exist and aren't ever likely to. In many cases, social media strategies are predominantly idea driven. They are often highly orchestrated by the clients themselves, creative PR and digital agencies and are judged on different success criteria than performance marketing campaigns. But the communications planner can and needs to play a role.

Here are five tips on what I've seen that works well when developing social media campaigns.

People want to hear from real people. As far as social media is concerned, users gravitate toward transparency. People would rather hear from real people. Putting a face on social media really helps. Tony Hsieh, the chief executive officer of online shoe store Zappos.com, personally tweets and has some 1.7 million followers on Twitter.[3]

Best Buy's Twelpforce has real employees dispensing advice via Facebook and YouTube. This is a great example of mobilizing the workforce to emphasize their point of difference with competitors such as Wal-Mart and Amazon: their people and their customer service.

Great content is king of the social media world too. The adage of television advertising is that people love watching animals and kids. Two YouTube sensations, Cadbury's drum-playing gorilla and Evian's roller-skating babies, seem to back this up.

Social media starts with an idea. It can come from a clever insight. Think Burger King's campaign on Facebook in which it rewarded customers with a free Whopper if they unfriended people. The idea drew on the high number of unwanted friend requests on the social media site.

At the moment, the best social ideas are coming from the creative (digital and nondigital) agency teams and for this reason: they are more likely to be the initiators of social media solutions. However, I believe the media agency is equally able to develop these ideas.

Seed and amplify the content. If a brand can generate content professionally, or even take advantage of user-generated content, the skill of the media team is in promoting the content, particularly among influencers. Seeding and amplifying might involve placing it in appropriate paid locations or promoting it through other media outlets or generating participation. For example, HBO's *True Blood* promoted its minisodes, three- to four-minute original-content episodes shot and written by creator Allan Ball, on Yahoo! TV before placing them on its Facebook fan page and HBO.com.

Another strategy is encouraging the online community to create content and share it. To encourage teenagers to stop smoking, the American Legacy Foundation used social networks to create advocates to share facts about cigarettes. For example, chemicals in cigarettes are also found in hair removal cream, which prompted the creation of a "hair mail" widget. Targets were set for the spread of viral films and website traffic.

Use social media websites as a brand destination; utilize insights of the community and technology to make a more relevant and involved experience. As people spend more time on social networking sites, such as MySpace and Facebook, marketers can supplement and in some cases replace their own branded websites by channeling social media sites as a brand destination. They do this to connect with consumers in an environment that consumers are more likely to visit. Starbucks, for instance, is deeply immersed in the Facebook experience. The coffee giant launched a Facebook app that allows customers to manage their Starbucks cards.

As with any marketing campaign, it is vital to understand the target audience and the role that social media plays in their lives and online behavior.

Of course, personal data is highly visible in social networks. USA Network, a cable channel owned by NBC Universal, promoted its detective drama *In Plain Sight* with that in mind. The series is about a witness protection program, and USA Network developed a Facebook widget that gave users a series of clues about a particular Facebook friend by gradually revealing the friend's personal information; the idea was to guess the identity of the friend.

Swedish furniture maker IKEA used one of Facebook's most popular functions, photo tagging—in which users are notified when they are identified in an uploaded photo—to promote the opening of a new store in Malmo, Sweden. The company created a Facebook profile for the store manager and posted photos of the IKEA showrooms. Whoever was first to tag his name and the items in the pictures won them. The idea was an interesting way to encourage people to tell their friends about the deals.

Focus less on measurement and more on what the brand is attempting to achieve. While online campaigns offer marketers the ability to reap an abundance of data and metrics, the focus should be first on developing good ideas that resonate with consumers and then on building out the campaign to deliver the communication goals and brand strategy. Then seek to maximize the visibility and reach of the campaign.

This is still a relatively young medium. Trying to overmeasure too early in a medium that is still evolving may stunt its potential. I asked Jeff Hayzlett, then chief marketing officer of Kodak, a fairly progressive company in terms of social media, how he was measuring it. He dismissed measuring social media, saying, "I measure my sales, brand recall and intent. That's what's important to me."[4]

EMPLOYING DIGITAL TACTICS

One of the principal roles of an online strategy is to identify the Consumer Pathway stage the communications are meant to address. To illustrate how digital has been particularly effective, see figure 10.1 for examples of how digital addressed a brand media communications need at different stages of the Consumer Pathway. Some examples that follow show how digital played a meaningful role in the communications. This is by no means an exhaustive list, but my goal is to inspire ideas for campaigns you're planning.

Given the astonishing pace of change in the digital world, I'm sure these will be outdated in no time. That's what makes this discipline so exciting.

FIGURE 10.1

Awareness	Involvement	Active consideration	Purchase	Consumption	Relationship / building	Advocacy
Premium banners, rich media incremental reach/reach niche audiences	Establish brand experiences that reinforce the brand idea	Search campaigns	Minimize cost per acquisition	Drive trial and sampling	Email marketing campaigns	Driving customer advocacy
Amplify / integrate the offline activity	Amplify events to a wider audience	Online campaigns to drive interest and traffic to branded site	Coupon offers online	Create brand utility that adds to the experience of the product	Build customer information & dialogue	
Seed word of mouth campaigns			ecommerce sites		Facebook fan pages	
Viral videos					Create content that drives branded community events	
Online video						

Example Digital Tactics

GENERATING AWARENESS

Premium Placements across High-Reach Portals

Online isn't necessarily the first medium that planners will think of when it comes to generating awareness. Television and newspapers are probably seen as lead media for that stage. However, the reach that online can now deliver is impressive. When GM launched its new Chevy Malibu in 2008, they bought a massive campaign of banners and embedded interactive ads on the home pages of Yahoo! MSN and AOL that extended across fifty high-traffic sites, including Weather.com, Amazon, Oprah.com and nytimes.com, as well as the main automotive sites. They *roadblocked*, or simultaneously displayed ads, on the major search engines. GM estimated that they delivered some 960 million impressions and reached nearly 90 percent of all US online users that day.

This strategy can be employed in niche markets and audiences, such as comic enthusiasts, Christian travelers or specialist B2B consumers, who can now be found and followed online with targeting technologies.

Amplify and Integrate with an Offline Campaign

Of course, no digital campaign runs completely isolated from other media. In many cases it complements or even amplifies an offline campaign. And no better example of that was the Doritos "Crash the Party" campaign for the 2008 Super Bowl. Doritos created a competition to come up with a Super Bowl ad. The prize was one million dollars if the ad earned the number-one spot on the USA Today Super Bowl Ad Meter. Brothers Dave and Joe Herbert won the prize. This became a phenomenal campaign that generated huge buzz for Doritos. The online component of this campaign included promotion of the competition and a site where the public could vote for their favorite ad, the winner becoming the Super Bowl ad. Very clever and definitely fitting into the "wish I had done that" category.

Seed Word of Mouth

One of digital's strong points is the ability to drive word-of-mouth communications. Online advertising's power to have consumers spread brand marketing messages is huge if a strong idea is developed. One example I really like is the campaign for the Karen Clifford Skin Cancer Society in the United Kingdom.

Awareness of skin cancer and its causes is very low in the United Kingdom, especially among youth. Research by the Teenage Cancer Trust found that 41 percent of teens never used sunblock and that 50 percent were not concerned about skin cancer.[5]

The Karen Clifford Skin Cancer Charity, known as Skcin, wanted to develop a campaign that would actively engage cynical teens. The idea was to communicate the dangers of skin cancer and, importantly, provide guidance to help avoid it. The vehicle was the creation of an elaborate hoax: a California-based company had developed technology allowing you to get a tan via your computer screen while viewing a website, www.computertan.com.

The campaign fooled users into visiting its site with the offer of free online tanning sessions. This was achieved through a program of newspaper, online and some out-of-home advertising. This was coordinated with a PR campaign and seeding on this program through key blogs.

When visitors first see the website, it shows tanning lamps for twenty seconds, but then the hoax is revealed. Images depicting the ravaging effects of skin cancer appear on the screen along with the number of people who die each day. Then the user is introduced to the nonprofit behind the campaign, Skcin.

It became an online phenomenon and notched over one million hits to the site within three months.[6] *(? nlg.)*

Viral Campaigns

In the world of viral media, creativity seriously counts. Most viral ad campaigns I know of have been created by the creative teams at the agency—you don't need to pay a media agency to upload a video to YouTube. However, with some twenty-four hours of video being uploaded every minute, the chances of being a viral success are pretty low. But it's a prize worth aiming for. The beauty of viral campaigns is that viewers find the content entertaining and amusing. The best viral campaigns some wouldn't even call advertising.

Brands such as Dove, Cadbury, Samsung, T-Mobile, Evian, Old Spice and blender retailer Blendtec have had much success with viral campaigns. Blendtec's legendary "Will It Blend?" campaign now totals over eighty individual executions in different media. The ad shows a man in a lab coat blending an oddball assortment of products, including an Apple iPhone.

Campaigns such as Old Spice's spot featuring the model Isaiah Mustafa and Cadbury's "Gorilla on the Drums" benefited from the thirty-second versions running as television spots. There are strategies to seed video into locations that can improve the chances of success, but as I said, creativity really rules the roost here.

BUILDING INVOLVEMENT

Building brand involvement as explained in chapter 3 moves beyond awareness to create experiences or occasions that make consumers more familiar with or favorable to brands.

Create brand experiences that reinforce the brand proposition. This can be done multiple ways in digital. One approach is to create more interaction and be more relevant to the consumer. Another is extending the television creative. Liberty Insurance did both of those with the following campaign.

Liberty Mutual Insurance

Insurance is one of the most competitive fields out there. The big guns Geico, Allstate, Progressive and State Farm spend millions on television ad campaigns.

Liberty Mutual took a completely different tack, choosing to associate itself with the idea of social responsibility. The multiplatform social awareness campaign was called "The responsibility project." The seeds of the campaign began with a television ad showing people doing good deeds like sharing an umbrella or letting someone else into a car parking spot.

Each person on the receiving end of a random act of kindness performs his or her own, creating a chain reaction. The spot was called "What Goes Around."

As Hill Holliday's executive vice president and chief media officer Baba Shetty said, the agency had to build on the concept in social media as the concept evolved. "The audience loved that spot, which presented a world-view of people doing the right thing," he added.[7]

On the Responsibility Project website, people could post videos and write about people doing kind things such as changing a tire for a stranger. When the site was launched, searching on "responsibility" showed the site's ranking as high as 6 out of some 247 million possible results. The website attracted 1.4 million unique visitors in its first nine months. The best result of all was that the company's consumer brand tracking showed an incredible 18 percent increase in people's appraisal of Liberty Mutual. The campaign's success underscores the power of social media to unleash people's natural inclination to do good and share the positive.

What made it work was the ease with which the elements of the campaign could be located and shared. "All the online pieces had been there for a while, but the scale of this campaign would not have been possible even a couple of years ago," says Shetty.[8]

Amplifying an Experiential Event

Another tactic I've seen done well by a number of brands is taking experiential marketing activities and amplifying them virally.

In the past, sponsored events were experienced only by those who attended. And stunts were employed in the hope of securing PR. The internet has helped create owned media content that can be discovered and distributed to a wider audience more economically.

T-Mobile in the UK staged such an event at London's Liverpool Street station. Employing 350 dancers to spontaneously break out into a dance routine, they filmed them and the reaction of hundreds of commuters and then uploaded the footage onto YouTube, drip feeding it over the subsequent weeks.

People picked up on it and began filming their own dance routines and sharing them with their friends through their social media networks.

T-Mobile's agency aggregated the best, worst and oddest clips of dancing onto T-Mobile's YouTube branded channel.

The video has been watched more than sixteen million times and has generated twelve thousand comments. The popularity of the campaign with consumers translated into strong sales. Handset sales increased 22 percent during launch week.[9]

INCREASING ACTIVE CONSIDERATION

Using Online Search to Increase Active Consideration

What do you want consumers to do as a result of seeing your advertising? Ideally, they purchase the product or put the brand on their shopping list. But more commonly, a brand wants to prompt consumers' consideration and research of the product, possibly by visiting the website or checking out reviews, articles or comparison sites. And that's where online search is one of the most powerful media in increasing active consideration. Search facilitates getting brands on the shopping list and guides the decision-making process for the purchase. Paid search is widely used for ecommerce or to drive traffic to websites, but using search at a campaign level is increasingly common. One of the reasons for this is that consumers are multitasking with media. Sixty percent of Americans go online while watching television.[10] Television advertising is the single biggest driver of search (see figure 10.2).[11]

We know from working with our pharmaceutical clients that one of the most desirable outcomes of consumers' seeing their advertising is for consumers to go on the internet to search for information about a health condition or a drug. The sheer size of the television-viewing audience and the curiosity that a thirty-second television ad engenders makes it the premiere channel for driving viewers to perform a search engine query.

Word of mouth, on the other hand, is not a mass advertising channel, although it can have large numbers. We discussed in chapter 6 how creating

FIGURE 10.2

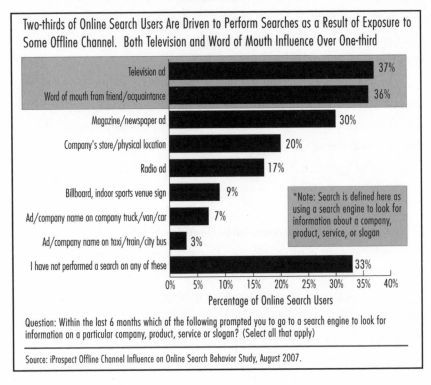

Two-thirds of Online Search Users Are Driven to Perform Searches as a Result of Exposure to Some Offline Channel. Both Television and Word of Mouth Influence Over One-third

Channel	Percentage
Television ad	37%
Word of mouth from friend/acquaintance	36%
Magazine/newspaper ad	30%
Company's store/physical location	20%
Radio ad	17%
Billboard, indoor sports venue sign	9%
Ad/company name on company truck/van/car	7%
Ad/company name on taxi/train/city bus	3%
I have not performed a search on any of these	33%

*Note: Search is defined here as using a search engine to look for information about a company, product, service, or slogan

Percentage of Online Search Users

Question: Within the last 6 months which of the following prompted you to go to a search engine to look for information on a particular company, product, service or slogan? (Select all that apply)

Source: iProspect Offline Channel Influence on Online Search Behavior Study, August 2007.

conversations was an important Brand Media Strategy. Supporting those efforts with paid search is an important part of capturing and converting the response.

Why Paid Search?

My observation is that many clients probably underinvest in paid search. It's easy to think that if consumers can find their site via unpaid, or natural, search, why bother with paid? Because paid search adds value in several levels.

It Helps Build the Brand

Paid search increases brand awareness and brand intent. Research by Google and MetrixLab revealed that the combination of exposure to paid search and a resultant click on a link increased campaign awareness by 20 percent and branding measures by 19 percent. And because paid search marketers pay only for the click, consumer exposure to the branding, which does not get clicked, is a bonus.[12]

Paid and Natural Searches Deliver Different Users

Cast the widest net. Research suggests that consumers arriving via paid search are further down the Consumer Pathway. Paid search visitors are 61 percent more likely to make a purchase than via natural search and to gather information and to look for deals.[13]

Prevent Poaching Traffic

Web measurement firm Hitwise suggests that leading ecommerce brands lose one in seven potential visitors to competitive brand search.[14]

Branded Destination Sites

Websites, microsites or brand presence on social media sites are all tools that aid active brand consideration. Most often, the role of the media team is to drive users to the website. However, being a communications planner in my book gives you permission to have a point of view on all the elements of the communications mix, including the brand destination site.

When reviewing a brand's site and its effectiveness, I always ask myself four questions:

Does it extend your brand? Does it have a point of view, a personality, a differentiated proposition? How does it help project the brand attributes and qualities?

Does it answer your prospects' most asked questions? Remember, the website is primarily for driving consideration or ecommerce. Therefore it needs to address questions potential customers might ask, to convince them of the brand.

Does it help you grow your prospects or contact list? Does the website help encourage further interaction? Does it encourage you to provide details for further contact?

Does it convert your prospects into customers? Lastly, does it move consideration to the next stage of the Consumer Pathway?

DRIVING PURCHASE

Online performance marketing through search, online display, affiliate programs or ad networks is the bread and butter of a digital media planning and buyer team. Optimizing and executing digital direct response programs are where the digital rubber hits the road. The focus of these media campaigns is primarily based on cost per click or cost per acquisition results. This is where digital teams bring a level of accountability and return on investment that few other channels can match.

Electronic coupon, or ecoupon, distribution is becoming a more popular means of distributing discounts or gift incentives to customers. The benefit over paper versions is the cost efficiency as well as the ability to put the coupons with the right offers in customers' hands. These can be pushed to customers via email or promoted or accessed via specific sites.

Mobile commerce, or m-commerce, also offers opportunities to drive sales. In August 2009 Pizza Hut launched an app that allowed consumers to order home delivery via their iPhone. Within just two weeks it had one hundred thousand downloads from the App Store. Customers use the app to order Pizza Hut menu items directly from their mobile devices using an intuitive touch screen interface. One feature I thought was fun was the exploding pizza when an overeager pizza customer adds too many toppings. Toppings go flying across the screen and a message tells the customer to use fewer toppings. Pizza Hut also gives consumers a way to pass the time as they wait for their order with a game called Pizza Hut Racer.

CONSUMPTION

Digital can even drive consumption or enhance the customer experience.

MyStarbucksIdea is a platform that encourages customers to share, discuss and vote on new ideas. Integrating social media components into print ads, they invite consumers to create their own media and spread the brand's story through Twitter, Facebook and other channels.

Starbucks used this site to help launch Starbucks instant coffee. The company staged a two-week, cross-country road trip with comedienne Erin Foley and Starbucks resident tweeter Brad Nelson. A film crew trailed the fourteen-state road trip and produced a series of quirky websites about car travel and caffeine. It helped to establish credibility in the market and drove trial. On the Facebook page alone there were more than 240,000 requests for samples.[15]

Nike, as discussed in chapter 2, is a brand that has not just developed a digital strategy but built brands and products for a digital world. One great example of how they did this was Nike+. R/GA chief Bob Greenberg explains, "Brands need to break away from the mentality of the 'campaign idea' and conceive ideas rooted in utility and value."[16] The Nike agency advocates technology that enables companies to build systems and applications that blur the line between product and marketing.

People track and share their runs on a Nike+ social networking web interface. Nike's Human Race recruits and connects participants and sets up city and country challenges. A Nike+ app allows runners to personalize copies of a Human Race commemorative book with their own photos.

In 2008 an incredible 780,000 runners in 30 countries participated in the race, and the publicity was largely accomplished without paid media. Nike's Ballers Network is a Facebook app that basketball players use to find pick-up games and manage their leagues.

For Nike Sparq R/GA created more than sixty training videos dedicated to football, basketball, soccer and women's sports. The product's market share has gone from 48 percent in the United States in 2006 to 61 percent in 2008.

RELATIONSHIP BUILDING

Online has been used numerous ways to maintain a dialogue and relationship with customers. The most common is customer-relationship-management, or eCRM, programs, which rely heavily on building a customer information database and consistent communications via email. I work with a retail client that built a customer database in little more than twelve months and has added literally tens of millions of dollars to their bottom line, first by establishing a relationship and then by providing customized and timely offers.

Social networks, forums, groups and blogs have been infiltrated by eCRM. Just about every brand now has fan pages on Facebook and a Twitter address. Of course, not every brand has millions of fans or followers. The most important need for these sites is content. Whether created by the brand or fans, content needs to be useful, entertaining and regularly updated. The other important aspect is recruitment of fans. I've seen fan sites that were heavily promoted through press releases, but they have only three hundred to four hundred fans, which for some companies is about the size of the marketing department! Promoting and recruiting fans is a must.

One great example of promotion of a brand community site is Visa's launch of its Go Biz program aimed at small-business owners. The digital campaign focused on how Visa Business helps businesses manage their finances better than using checks. The campaign includes professionally shot webumentaries of real businesspeople telling their story via www. visa.com/gobiz and discussing issues such as managing their financial matters. The videos were also posted on YouTube. The website invites users to join Visa's Business Network, a social network of over one hundred thousand members.[17] The network provided giveaways of one-hundred-dollar Facebook ad credits and seventy-five-dollar Yahoo! Search Marketing credits to its members. Other media included online banners on Entrepreneur, MSN, Yahoo! and AOL.com; national network radio; and trade print advertising.

AMPLIFYING ADVOCACY

Word of mouth is well covered in chapter 6, where we explored how digital and social media fuels brand conversations.

OBAMA 2008—A BREAKTHROUGH FOR DIGITAL MEDIA

Digital provides communication solutions to drive the Brand Media Strategy across the spectrum of the Consumer Pathway, from awareness to advocacy. Importantly, even though they are highly creative and highly effective, these communication solutions must also have a clear role as part of the overall Brand Media Strategy. This requires digital to address specific brand needs on the Consumer Pathway. Solutions can cross the spectrum of digital media, from search to social, from en masse to one-on-one. Digital as a channel continues to be an opportunity to innovate and use technology and ideas to create interactive experiences.

I've made a few references to Barack Obama's presidential campaign in this book. Obama's campaign was a significant mark in the marketing industry. Senator Obama's campaign received recognition by *Advertising Age*, being awarded its top marketing campaign of 2008. It was a campaign that employed digital in several areas: website, social media, mobile and email. It scaled personalized marketing through digital. It was a campaign that changed the game and helped transform the way the industry thought about digital marketing. For these reasons, it's worth concluding this chapter with a case study of the campaign.

CASE STUDY: OBAMA'S SOCIAL MEDIA STRATEGY: YES WE CAN

In January 2009, America inaugurated its first African American president. It was the culmination of the most fascinating political marketing campaign in decades.

The nation's so-called first tech president had a group of dedicated staffers who understood how to use online networks and Facebook-style tools to recruit, energize and engage volunteers. Of course, that didn't mean abandoning the bullhorn of traditional media to address voters with the wider message. The campaign, after all, made a media buy in Super Bowl 2008 to promote a spot called "Join."

Political campaigns had traditionally focused on using television advertising to target undecided voters and to respond quickly to attacks. But Obama's social media strategy always linked the marketing to action: a call to get actively involved in the campaign, to fundraise, to vote. "We were starting from scratch. We knew we had to get millions of people involved to have any chance of winning the election," said David Plouffe, the campaign manager.[18]

"This campaign could not have been run 10 years ago," said senior campaign strategist Jim Margolis, who works at ad agency GMMB. "It was fueled by the Internet and it was fueled by people's involvement and activism."[19] The Obama campaign team's new media strategies took political marketing to new levels, employing Facebook, Twitter, personalized email communications and texting to leverage his supporter base to persuade voters.

I analyzed the Obama and Clinton campaigns in an article for *Advertising Age*.[20] Obama scored more positively in his use of social media when countering his opponent, Hillary Clinton, who did better in traditional media with such negative efforts as the "3:00 A.M. phone call" ad campaign, which raised the question of Obama's readiness for office.

Although Obama had more money in his war chest, his team continued to portray Obama as the underdog. When Hillary Clinton lent her own campaign five million dollars, the Obama team responded by sending out an email to his million-plus supporters the next day. That email solicitation read, "We need to match this quickly, can you help?" Within twenty-four hours respondents had donated $8 million.

When it came to social media, Obama far outranked Clinton. At the start of her campaign, Clinton was featured heavily on blogs and was an early proponent of YouTube. Clinton produced a spot set in a New Jersey diner that was a spoof of the series finale of *The Sopranos*. However,

Obama decisively won the battle for the user-generated media channel. Nearly three times as many videos were uploaded by the Obama camp as the Clinton camp, with ten times more views. The viral impact of the "I Got a Crush . . . on Obama" video by Obama Girl generated more than sixteen and a half million views on YouTube.[21] Obama could also count on one million Facebook and MySpace friends.

The Obama camp had a greater understanding of the power of the relative newcomer Twitter to deliver focus group comment in real time. As my *Ad Age* article pointed out back in June 2008, Barack Obama had 33,069 followers on Twitter while Hillary Clinton had 4,019.[22] But the big difference was not in their respective numbers of followers but in the people *they* followed: Obama's camp followed 33,000 people on Twitter (enabling them to hear what people were saying about the campaign and the issues); Clinton's camp didn't follow anybody. As Twitter has grown, so has Obama's volume of followers. The official BarackObama Twitter feed twitter.com/BARACKOBAMA had 4.2 million people signed up as of June 2010.

The Obama campaign's ability to create personal relationships via mass-marketing techniques characterized his Brand Media Strategy. The employment of digital media channels—notably his website, use of social media and email marketing—helped gain younger voters' support and proved effective in fundraising, a critical factor in sustaining a heavy marketing effort.

The campaign set up a website called MyBarackObama, which provided organizers with the kind of information they might need: legal data about financial contributions, downloadable voter registration forms and forums for separate groups to share best practices and organize events. It also had a rapid response area, where anyone could fact-check statements made by candidates or media outlets.

When the campaign concluded, the website had hosted some two million profiles and four hundred thousand blogs, and had raised some thirty million dollars via seventy thousand pages. MyBarackObama.com still exists and is operated by Organizing for America as a way to further grassroots activity and effect political change.

The campaign didn't employ social media for its own sake but to achieve goals such as fund-raising, creation of email distribution lists, advance work and, most importantly, establishment of a nationwide organization.

Pete Snyder, cofounder of New Media Strategies, a company that creates online word-of-mouth marketing for major corporations, says, "They made online the central nervous system for their organization; smart brands are going to start doing this. The ripple effect will be felt for years to come."[23]

The campaign was a turning point for the industry as it illustrated the value of making digital central to communications. It was integral in driving pledges but also in terms of its widespread influence. Digital did not live out there on its own; it was fully integrated into a broader mainstream media campaign.

QUESTIONS TO ASK FOR A BRAND MEDIA STRATEGY'S USE OF DIGITAL

1. What stage of the Consumer Pathway is digital media addressing?
2. What and where can digital add to the campaign?
3. How do the digital tactics integrate with other elements in the plan?
4. How should you measure the performance of digital?

CHAPTER 11

EXECUTION IS THE X-FACTOR

BRINGING THE BRAND MEDIA STRATEGY TO LIFE

The most important part of a strategy is executing it. A good strategy with great tactics is always going to beat a great strategy with poor tactics. Consumers don't experience strategy; they see and hear the brand through media. They view a television spot, content on the internet or a billboard on the highway, and they respond accordingly.

There's no room in the communications planner's world for fluffy ideas and theory. And while it's important to have a clearly identified outcome and a focused plan, what's crucial is how the Brand Media Strategy is activated in the media world. To punctuate this point, at Optimedia we adopted the mantra "Strategy, brilliantly executed," because we believe and know that you can't separate the two.

This chapter is dedicated to bringing the strategy to life. It explains how we execute strategies through media solutions and how to bring the activation ideas to life.

GETTING THE BEST WORK
FROM YOUR MEDIA PARTNERS

At one point in my career, I left the media agency world to start a digital marketing venture, and I found myself in the role of selling to and performing services for media agencies for the first time. To be honest, it was a bit of a shock to the system. The agencies we worked with supplied terrible briefs. There was little or no information or insight into the clients' business goals. No agency ever shared the brand's communications strategy or even indicated there was one. There were no key performance indicators; there was no communication of desired outcomes of the campaigns. There was little openness to adopting a different angle. The agencies just wanted a response to standard requests for proposals (RFPs).

And they wanted it yesterday—actually, last week. Most importantly, they wanted it at the lowest cost per thousand or cost per click possible.

If I had a dime for every time an agency planner or buyer said, "Can you bring us some innovative, never-been-done-before ideas," I could retire!

I developed a renewed respect for the professionalism of the women and men in the media sales community; they are better people than I. In the end, our sales director wisely started excluding me from meetings with media agencies. He told me it wasn't good for business to be telling agencies what they should or shouldn't be doing, even if I was right.

Many times the proposals went nowhere. In fact, a media vendor I recently spoke to told me that positive responses to RFPs happened less than 5 percent of the time. All those rejected RFPs seem such an unnecessary waste of time and resources for everyone.

By and large, agencies got the work they deserved. Maybe every once in a while they got something great, but they usually ended up with a cut-and-paste solution—hardly the ingredient for brilliant, award-winning, market-moving results. It was a shame because, as an outside vendor, we had the ability to help them do some amazing things.

FROM STRATEGY TO ACTIVATION

Once the Brand Media Strategy is developed, the next step is to translate it into an insightful brief for the activation teams—potential partners that are a source of ideas or assets that can help implement brand communications in paid, earned or owned media forms.

They include the specialist buying teams at the agency for broadcast, print and out-of-home media as well as digital planners and buyers who operate across channels such as display, search, social media and mobile.

Specialist marketing channel experts and partners can also include event marketing, branded entertainment, custom content producers, stunt or live activations and below-the-line efforts such as marketing PR and shopper marketing.

Media companies are part of a communications planner's activation team, as are the client's nominated agency partners, or internal integrated marketing teams. Those can include creative, digital, PR and marketing activation people.

THE BRIEFING: GARBAGE IN, GARBAGE OUT

We've all heard that well-worn cliché "garbage in, garbage out." Well, the reason it's a cliché is because people keep using it. They keep using it because so often it's true.

The briefing provides the fuel for good ideas to take off. Too often, briefings are seen as a chore to get off the task list as expediently as possible. A briefing should be a source of inspiration and opportunity. It's the fun part of our business: a venue to create and innovate. But great work isn't a random exercise in ideation. It should be an important and well-orchestrated function at the agency.

The briefing to the activation teams should be wide enough to solicit a suitcase full of ideas but narrow enough to set out clear expectations of where to play and how to win.

Great communication ideas and brand media thinking come from collaboration and being disciplined about organizing people. Everyone can bring great ideas to the table and most people want to contribute.

ACTIVATION IS A TWO-STEP PROCESS

Decide on the big idea, or central communicating idea, that anchors the plan. This allows the planner to develop the media activations. Does this integrate the communications across multiple media channels? For instance, Pepsi's 2008 "Wake-up" campaign used the concept of "Stop the yawn" as its central communicating idea.

Develop tactical programs with the activation teams that expand and support the central communicating idea. This involves developing ideas with the execution teams, as well as developing RFPs to brief partners. This includes work with digital and social media partners, branded entertainment companies or experiential marketing companies to develop events or content. For example, Pepsi set up "Stop the Yawn" video game arcades, and consumers used Pepsi-branded Max water guns to squirt the yawns away as part of its "Wake-up" campaign.

DEVELOPING THE CENTRAL COMMUNICATING IDEA

The big idea is developed out of the consumer insight work, which we discussed in chapter 5.

There's no one right answer for how to establish the central communicating idea. Here's a list of steps that I've found useful:

COME UP WITH MULTIPLE ALTERNATIVE IDEAS

It's easy to become married to just one idea and stick with it. But you need to have alternatives so you can leave an idea behind if it isn't strong enough or it's not executable or it's just unaffordable.

Having alternative ideas is the best way of testing the quality of the first idea, because more often than not, the first idea is not the best. I've seen it happen often: agencies get stuck on an idea, and their effort goes to selling the idea rather than testing its efficacy.

DON'T STOP AT THE A-HA MOMENT

An idea is never fully baked at the start. Look at ways to fine-tune it, evolve it, torture test it. Make the idea bigger. I used to think that great creative ideas just happened in a moment of inspiration. Roger MacDonnell, a creative director who ran one of the first creative agencies I worked at, convinced me that great creativity comes from hard work and determination to continuously make the idea better.

GET EVERYONE TO OWN THE IDEA

I know there's a school of thought that says ideas are best if kept pure and unsullied by others. But an idea becomes more powerful if it doesn't belong to just one person. The team has to own it. A good test of an idea is when everyone wants to claim it.

That requires the planner to be open to everyone's views of how to improve the idea by letting different parties add to it. The communications process needs to be a collaborative team effort.

REALLY SELL THE IDEA

A great idea only ever happens if a client buys it. This is where creative agencies do a brilliant job. They don't toss out ideas to clients randomly. They put care and attention into crafting and presenting an idea. They produce impressive storyboards and mood tapes to help sell that idea. They treat it and present it as if it's the most important thing in the world. You're asking client representatives to stake their company's money on it and possibly their jobs, so make them feel they're betting on a sure thing.

It has to work across multiple platforms. Great ideas need to cross into multiple media, particularly digital, so don't let the origin of the idea limit its use.

TESTING THE CENTRAL COMMUNICATING IDEA

Once you develop several candidates for the central communicating idea, you need to test them. We need to apply the filters shown in figure 11.1 to judge whether an idea works.

The first filter is to determine if the idea is strategic. Does the central communicating idea address the communication objective? Will it enhance the desirable brand attributes, brand point of view, positioning? Does it capture or work off a target audience insight? Will consumers care? Dove's "Campaign for Real Beauty" lived up to the brand's global objective "to be

FIGURE 11.1

Testing the Central Communicating Idea	
Questions to Ask as You Develop the Central Communicating Idea	
Strategic	• Does it address the communication objective? • Will it enhance desirable brand attributes? • Is it in line with the brand's POV, positioning, and target audience?
Influential	• Can it cut through the clutter?
Simple	• Is it unique?
Ownable	• Can it help drive an emotional connection with the brand? • Does it address the consumer insight and motivational barriers?
Emotive	• How does it relate to these key points — Is it useful, is it entertaining, is it relevant?

Note: POV, point of view.

the preferred beauty brand of women who want to make the most of their natural beauty."[1] They saw this campaign as an opportunity to champion real women. Dove asked, What's the best way to get on their side? And Dove argued *their* case.

Will the idea be influential when it's executed? Most importantly, will it cut through the clutter of the category? Is it unexpected? Will it get attention? Surprises hold attention and interest. Is it counterintuitive? Is it something concrete that will help people understand and remember? The "Campaign for Real Beauty" worked well because it displaced the category convention of promoting *unattainable* beauty. The campaign celebrated the real beauty that comes in women of all sizes, shapes and colors. Dove's agencies chose to celebrate natural beauty, letting each woman make the most of the real her. No more models!

A third filter is simplicity. Is the idea focused, clear and simple to execute? Does it help people understand and remember? Define the core message in one simple and profound sentence. For Dove's "Campaign for Real Beauty," it was "to help make more women beautiful every day."

Is the idea ownable? Can you tell a story around the idea? Dove occupies the lucrative everyday premium slot in the skin and hair care category. This gave them permission to talk about beauty across a range of products. They could stick up for the everyday woman. Was the campaign idea unique? Yes— it broke new ground, and as a result got women around the world talking.

Finally, can it drive an emotional response? Can it connect with and be relevant to its audience? Dove's campaign played off the insight of "I'm tired of fake images of beauty. I want to take good care of the body I've got, making the most of the real me."

Once the central communicating idea has been run through these filters and is established, the second part of the activation process is to develop tactical programs with activation teams that expand and drive the central communicating idea. This involves developing RFPs to brief vendors, digital agencies, social media partners, branded entertainment companies and experiential marketing companies to develop programs and events.

One valuable means to develop these tactical programs is brainstorming.

FACILITATING IDEAS THROUGH BRAINSTORMING

If the strategy and insights are the fuel for ideas, then brainstorming is the combustion engine that sparks those ideas.

Brainstorming was popularized by an advertising guy, Alex Osborn, the "O" in BBDO.[2] Brainstorming is an important tool for generating ideas. Even more, it's a core task in an agency. I've always believed that the best part of advertising is coming up with ideas. I suspect that's what attracts a lot of young people to our profession. Brainstorming brings together two other important aspects of the agency business—collaboration and having fun. Hence, it's a process I like to encourage planners and buyers to participate in.

Anyone can participate, whatever the department. Even the most inexperienced or junior employee can come up with ideas. In fact, they are more likely to be better at it than most chief executive officers and senior managers, who tend to be more problem solvers and whose jobs revolve around managing order.

Instead, first-year planners or buyers are more likely to be creative and in tune with technology, and they're also heavy consumers of media and in touch with popular culture. They are more often the very consumers we chase.

HOW TO BRAINSTORM

Getting the most out of a brainstorming session starts with a good facilitator. A facilitator's job is to chair the meeting rather than have the ideas. A facilitator motivates and encourages creative thinking and keeps things moving.

Encourage participation and fun. Hey, it beats doing Excel spreadsheets and pivot tables for an hour or so! Keep it upbeat. Evaluating or criticizing ideas is a no-no. There will be plenty of time later to filter the ideas. It's also important to put everyone on equal footing; no one in a brainstorming session is more senior than the other participants.

Put together a diverse team. The team should include people with different strengths, life and work experiences and craft skills. Ideally, have people who don't work on the client's business, and even better try to include at least one person who doesn't work in the agency. Keep the tone upbeat, enthusiastic and creative. An optimum number for a brainstorming session is between six and ten people.

Focus on the quantity of ideas first. Quantity breeds quality. The more ideas, the higher the chance of moving off the obvious and current reference points to something new and never been done.

To create, the team needs a comfortable space. Have colorful cushions, rooms with lots of light, food and drink. Make sure to have a large bulletin board on a wall for attaching ideas and insights. This isn't a scientific process; it's an organic one.

Write it all down. Ideas should be submitted as headlines. Keep the ideas visible; perhaps capture them on flip charts or sticky notes. Circulate the notes after the meeting, in case the participants have ideas the next day.

Encourage idea building. Stretch what is discussed as far as possible to improve and sharpen the concepts. Encourage people to see how an idea could grow. Use comments like "That's a great idea; can anyone think of how we could build out that thought further?"

HARVESTING FOR GOOD IDEAS

An increasingly popular alternative to brainstorming is crowd sourcing. This involves throwing a question out on the web for the masses to solve.

Over the years it's become clearer to me that people from outside the agency or agency business offer a lot of value to creative exercises. Outsiders bring new perspectives and compensate for the blind spots of the target group (the fish is the last to notice the water). Diversity always pays.

Two obvious places to crowd-source ideas are Twitter and Facebook. Ask friends or followers for ideas.

I met some people at a conference who managed a website called OpenAd.net, which is a professional site that marketers and agencies use. The site accesses around 11,000 freelance creatives from around the world and offers to come up with fresh ideas for marketers and agencies. Clients can create a pitch online. If ideas are accepted, the originators and the site are paid.

THE INTEGRATED ACTIVATION BRIEF

The Brand Media Strategy is the foundation for the integrated activation brief (figure 11.2). The brief should provide core product and brand information and relevant consumer insights. The briefing explains what the communications plan needs to achieve. It also sets out the business and communication goals of the plan and the Consumer Pathway stages that the communications are to target.

FIGURE 11.2

THE INTEGRATED ACTIVATION BRIEF

Product and brand background

Who are the customers

The campaign's goals
- Business & communication goals
- What are we trying to achieve
- What stages of the Consumer Pathway are we trying to influence

The campaign strategy
- A central consumer, brand or business insight
- The central communicating idea or strategic platform
- The creative idea (if available)
- Areas of receptivity

Specific role of the channel identified

Metrics
- How will you measure success

Provide some initial tactics as guidelines

Budget options

Timing

The briefing details the central communicating idea, or overall strategic platform, and any viewpoint established on receptivity. It includes the potential role of each touch point in driving the communications: for instance, "We need television to get people to visit the website to find out more information."

The briefing defines the metrics for judging the plan and any initial tactics that the planning team has brainstormed. These are used as a guideline for further ideation or development. It also suggests the initial budget, which is subject to further refinement. And lastly, the briefing includes the timing of each element of the campaign.

THE INITIAL BRIEFING EXCHANGE

Activation ideas begin with an initial briefing exchange. This is a meeting between the planning and activation teams, who use the time to dissect, tear apart and re-create the brief, if necessary. We use it to torture test the central communicating idea. Does the team think it can play out across different media channels? The team checks whether the budget parameters make sense.

At this stage it's ideal to get a provisional sign-off on the strategy and touch-point recommendations from the client before doing specific briefing for activations and tactics. Develop a synergistic RFP that can be applied across different media partners and vendors, then list the initial partners to decide what platforms will be used.

Explain the requirements of the activation plan to the vendors; set expectations and a timetable for a response. Ask for initial ideas and package the proposal. Review the ideas and share the review with the entire team. Identify the best: the ideas that can work on a variety of media platforms. Judge the ideas against the strategy, the potential impact and coverage needs. Focus time, energy and budget on the handful of ideas that really break through. Finally, present the recommendations to the client and get sign-off so you can move on developing the idea platform in more depth.

CHALLENGES IN ACTIVATING THE BRAND MEDIA STRATEGY

Sometimes planners develop a communications strategy that the activation teams can't execute on. The Brand Media Strategy looks good on paper; it dovetails nicely with a powerful insight and the client really loves and agrees to the approach. But activation teams are left scratching their heads because they can't translate the strategy into something real.

One case I recall that illustrates this was when our agency, Optimedia, pitched the Payless ShoeSource account, the country's largest specialist shoe retailer. We developed an initial strategy that would leverage the retailer's goal of emotionally connecting with consumers through the democratization of fashion. A core insight we developed when we pitched this (in early April 2008, well before the recession's effects were felt) was that many women enjoy bragging about frugality. We saw an opportunity in getting new customers into the franchise by having customer fans be advocates.

One peripheral initiative Payless was implementing was www.ILove Shoes.com. Payless ShoeSource had acquired the URL but hadn't marketed it extensively. The web address featured in some of their print and point-of-sale materials. We decided that we were on to something and wanted to make "I love shoes" much more front and center with their media communications. So we came up with the central communicating idea of "Share the love."

Chris Pyne, our strategic planning director, and I loved it. We gave it the overnight test and loved it even more. We then briefed the idea to the broadcast, print and digital teams and asked them to come up with ideas to blow this idea out.

Conceptually, the idea worked nicely, and maybe because as chief executive I had given my seal of approval, the teams tried to be enthusiastic about it. They came back with some initial ideas, but they struggled to light it up. After about a week of seeing what came back, we killed it and found an alternative idea that worked much better in execution. It was a lesson that illustrated the importance of making sure that strategy can be executed. The happy ending was that we did win the pitch.

DEVELOPING MEDIA *AND* MESSAGE

Some of the best ideas come from media vendors. Because they are content creators, they know how to create what their audiences want to see and what's sticky. As we discussed in chapter 2, with the media business revenue model under pressure, media companies want to use their resources as ways to attract advertising revenues and market share by leveraging content. There are plenty of examples. AOL chief executive Tim Armstrong has positioned AOL as a content company first; investing resources in developing custom content for advertisers is a big part of their offering to marketers.

Time Warner set up its own division to handle custom specific marketing programs. NBC Universal has gone beyond its traditional role of broadcaster to marketing partner by establishing a creative department that helps produce brand marketing creative assets.

Media agencies are developing content too. WPP has Mindshare Entertainment, Starcom MediaVest Group has Liquid Thread, and our own agency launched its branded content division called NewCast.

INTERRUPTION VERSUS DISRUPTION

To some extent I agree that communication needs to be more relevant, sympathetic and entertaining to the consumer. But let's not forget that advertising is still advertising. The fact is that commercial breaks interrupt your television programs and your morning radio and compete for space on your msn.com home page. It has become very popular to advocate that advertising needs to move past the interruption model into one of permission.

In my view, there's nothing wrong with disrupting the attention of the consumer. Standing out is a prerequisite of executing a communications plan. The difference between a campaign that is ignored and one that gets noticed is an ad that is executed in a compelling and creative way. Ideally, that ad must involve and engage, and that's why the execution is so important. The role of the activation team is to push the envelope further.

Executing campaigns and promoting brands is a skill that's always in a state of flux. Ten years ago, the notion of television presenters having any connection to advertised brands would have been frowned upon, and even scorned. Now we watch MSNBC *Morning Joe* hosts drink Starbucks coffee and talk show hosts Jimmy Kimmel or Ellen DeGeneres perform live commercials. The Mark Burnett reality show *Survivor,* aired on CBS, broke ground in the world of brand integration when it wove in everything from Pontiacs to Doritos and Bud Light as prizes for those marooned on a desert island with little to eat.

Great execution strategies have a few things in common: They blur the line between content and advertising. They use technology. They're interactive and they create experiences and participation.

BLURRING THE LINE BETWEEN CONTENT AND ADVERTISING

One effective tactic in media is blending the advertising and content through program partnerships. Here are two examples of this from Turbo-Tax and NBC Universal and from HP and MTV Networks.

CASE STUDY: TURBOTAX AND NBC UNIVERSAL

In January 2010, NBC Universal executed the second year of promotions for TurboTax by featuring talent from the network's shows. The deal involved six NBC networks and featured actors from prime-time shows. For example, a cast member from *Community* talks about a deductible business lunch and a cast member from *Ghost Hunters* talks about tax advice while on a ghost hunt. The ad spots also aired in sports programming and at other times of day.

Mike Pilot, president of sales and marketing for NBC Universal, stated, "We know that connecting a client's brand to the equity of our content and our platforms sends engagement scores through the roof." He cites research the network undertook to evaluate viewer response to these program promotions.[3]

CASE STUDY: HP AND MTV NETWORKS

In the world of computers, there's Apple and there's everybody else. PCs were for office workers in suits and ties, while Apple Macs were for creative types. HP was very much the Johnny-come-lately to the style party.

In terms of technology, a Mac can't do anything more than a PC. What largely sets it apart is branding and design.

If HP wanted to ensure future business, it needed to target today the business leaders and style icons of tomorrow. The challenge their agency team faced was to make the PC cool again.

So how could HP make people perceive it as a cool, creative brand? Telling young people that HP had changed, that it had suddenly become stylish and desirable, wouldn't convince them. HP had to show them. The agency had to create a platform, an alternative reality if you will, that would show cool, creative and early adopters (the demographic many young people look to as trendsetters) that using HP's equipment could produce great creative work.

They partnered with MTV to show Millennials that the brand was relevant and accessible. The result was a multimedia reality show called *Engine Room*, in which sixteen of the most talented students from around the world competed in series of creative challenges, all using HP equipment.

First they needed candidates. The global campaign kicked off with an intensive television ad burst in North America, Latin America, Europe and Asia. The campaign asked people to submit their portfolios. A viral seeding strategy got under way with partners posting details of the campaign on relevant blogs and forums. Universities and design schools were targeted with posters to attract budding digital artists. Over two thousand applicants, from over 110 countries, competed for the sixteen coveted places in the competition.[4] These seven creative challenges, ranging from animation, filmmaking and sound mixing to web and graphic design, would showcase the power and style of HP's new product range.

The young artists now had a worldwide stage, and they received mentorship and critiques from a wide range of industry leaders, including iconic musicians, Hollywood directors, pioneering graphic designers and the Guggenheim Museum's chief curator.[5] The final challenge asked MTV viewers to enter the *Engine Room* notebook design contest to create their own HP special-edition notebook for 2009. The competition invited artists from around the world to submit their best designs for a chance to have their art appear on the next special-edition HP notebook.

The campaign changed young people's attitudes toward HP. In a proprietary global study, research showed that after viewers watched MTV's *Engine Room* the message of creativity was so strong that more young people associated HP with the sentiment "can do creative things on their PCs" than they did with Apple. (HP got 58 percent of the vote versus 51 percent for rival Apple.)[6]

The *Engine Room* site was bombarded. Almost eight hundred thousand unique visitors came to the site. The content-seeding strategy on blogs was so relevant that the links achieved a whopping 12 percent click-through rate, the number of links clicked divided by the number of link impressions.[7]

TECHNOLOGY: TURNING ADVERTISING INTO A UTILITY

Innovative use of technology can often be the difference between what stands out and what fades into the background.

Moxie Interactive and 20th Century Fox Studios personalized promotions for their 2008 holiday movie *Marley & Me* by creating a website that invited consumers to have the main character in the movie, the dog Marley, fetch holiday gift ideas from various websites. At the center of the site is a search box that has Marley delivering on gift suggestions, while another allows visitors to buy tickets.

CASE STUDY: CREATING IRRESISTIBLE EXPERIENCES

I've long admired how Unilever was able to transform itself from a predominantly television brand marketer to one that consistently shows imagination and deft in becoming an experience-led brand marketer across their brand portfolio. Nowhere is that more evident than with grooming brand Axe (or Lynx as it is known in the UK, Ireland and Australia).

Launching its new body spray fragrance "Dark Temptation" in 2008, they worked off insight work they had undertaken with women across 13 different countries. They unearthed a universal international truth that women find chocolate irresistible. They developed a central communicating idea of "irresistible as chocolate." This platform became the central idea to execute experiences across its markets. The creative agency developed this into a core idea of a chocolate man featured in the advertising.

The media agency Mindshare developed an international campaign creating experiences around the brief of "irresistible as chocolate." For example, in France 200,000 guys received "chocolate nibbles & licks" from girls on social networking site Skyrock.com. In the UK, they challenged British guys to test their pick-up skills by asking out women armed with just a bar of chocolate. In Brazil, they created an interactive online video game "The Dark Temptation," which involved a chocolate man being chased by women. And in India, the brand created a chocolate fashion show attended by the fashion press and celebrities.

Nick Waters, leader of Mindshare EMEA, said: "Axe Dark Temptation is a wonderful example of taking a strong central idea and adapting it to resonate locally across the region."[8]

Axe's Dark Temptation was the fourth-most-successful launch in the company's twenty-five-year history, surpassing all major global and European sales goals.[9]

Another great example of using online to develop consumer experiences was that of 20th Century Fox using digital to drive experiences around *The Simpsons Movie* to activate interest and attendance.

CASE STUDY: *THE SIMPSONS MOVIE*— BLURRING MEDIA AND REALITY

There is no more hotly contested market than the box office. New big-budget movies from Hollywood's largest production companies slug it out every week to see which movies will have a big opening weekend and which will be also-rans. Being number one for an opening weekend can be the difference between making one hundred million dollars and losing one hundred million dollars. Few movies survive long after a weak opening. *The Simpsons Movie* had one advantage: a big preexisting base of loyal fans. Yet the franchise was almost twenty years old, and it had no guarantee that its popular thirty-minute format would entice fans to pay eight dollars to watch a full-length movie.

Relying on advertising that focused on the popularity of the show or its characters to drive ticket sales would be a mistake, 20th Century Fox Studios realized. Had they done that, a simple television campaign on high-rated shows would have given them all the reach they needed to get the word out. Instead, they took advantage of the special opportunities created by emerging media. Their goal was to create a level of involvement with *The Simpsons* that went way beyond awareness of a new movie launch. By carefully manipulating the contextual opportunities presented by both digital and experiential media, Fox made the launch of *The Simpsons Movie* less like a typical movie launch and more like a cultural event.

For starters, Fox created fun television commercials and an engaging website. The site had lots of cool stuff, from the usual (for example, computer wallpapers and screen savers) to some silly yet surprisingly addictive games, complete with lots of "D'oh" and "Aye Carumba!" sound effects. It had a virtual tour of Springfield and a tool that let you create your own *Simpsons* avatar—just the sort of thing to get *Simpsons* fans engaged. But understanding context often means understanding that the people you want to reach will not necessarily go to your site. So Fox created a cross-promotion on Burger King's site where people could submit a photo and "Simpsonize" themselves. This was a viral application that was fun to do and share whether you were a *Simpsons* fanatic or not. Where the campaign really shined, however, was in its use of the web and the real world to turn context on its head.

Three ideas from the campaign are outstanding examples of reinventing the way people relate to media in its broadest sense. The first was an online contest that pitted fourteen different American cities named Springfield for the honor of being named *the* Springfield of *Simpsons* fame, giving the winner the right to hold the movie's premiere. The contest got the populations of these cities engaged and became a public relations extravaganza, with the contest and results covered by sponsor *USA Today* and news organizations around the country. When little Springfield, Vermont, beat the likes of sizable Springfield, Illinois, the residents of the winning town were described by *USA Today* as being in a *Simpsons* "frenzy."[10]

The second idea was an online campaign in partnership with JetBlue Airways. As one might expect, different Simpsons became spokespersons for different JetBlue destinations. But the campaign started to bend reality by having the show's corporate mogul Montgomery Burns take over the JetBlue chairman's blog. The hijacked blog led off as follows: "Hi I'm Montgomery Burns, Here's my newest attempt at robbing a man of his livelihood. I have temporarily taken over David Neeleman's blog as I believe I have more efficient ways to run this airline. I could crush him like an ant."

The third, and perhaps most spectacular, contextual idea was a joint promotion with 7-Eleven. Eleven 7-Eleven stores around America were physically transformed into Kwik-E-Marts (patterned after the show's convenience store helmed by Apu Nahasapeemapetilon), complete with loads of *Simpsons*-based products. All of the signage inside and out was changed. For people on the street or anyone stopping by for their morning cup of coffee, the world was just a little bit different. The line between fantasy and reality had been crossed. They not only knew there was a movie coming out but were deeply engaged in the *Simpsons* experience. People didn't have to be *Simpsons* fanatics to be caught up in the amusement and to feel that life would be a little more fun if they went to the movie.

Fox's creativity in challenging the usual uses of media, and even reality, led to tremendous results. The film earned seventy-four million dollars for its opening weekend. It was the third-highest nonsequel opening of all time. Had this animated movie, with its quirky sense of humor, looked at media in the traditional way, or even used digital media in a noncreative way, there is a good chance that only *Simpsons* fans would have shown up.

QUESTIONS TO ASK ABOUT EXECUTING THE BRAND MEDIA STRATEGY

1. From the executions, can you guess what the big idea is?
2. How does this strategy differentiate the product from competitors' products in the category?
3. Does the media plan amplify the creative campaign?
4. Does this campaign stand out, disrupt?

CHAPTER 12

MEASUREMENT AND METRICS

MAKING THE BRAND MEDIA
STRATEGY ACCOUNTABLE

In a world that is drowning in data, knowing what to ignore is as important as knowing what to consider. . . . Over-reliance on metrics is stifling marketing. Justifying marketing's value only through metrics results in an over-emphasis on metrics . . . the numbing by numbers. . . . Do not use metrics to justify; use metrics to guide continuous improvement.

—Larry Light, former global chief marketing officer, McDonald's, now chief executive officer, Arcature[1]

EMBRACING MEASUREMENT

I face a tough challenge with this chapter: how to make measurement and metrics interesting enough for a planner to want to read it!

Return-on-investment (ROI) numbers for many communications planners is a bit like going to the dentist: something you need to check in with regularly but not something you look forward to. But measuring effectiveness for the Brand Media Strategy is more than just a box-ticking exercise or a cosmetic procedure like teeth whitening. It's the very core of communications planning.

One of the most fundamental points of communications planning is *not* whether the campaign sold more product or grew market share. It's about understanding where and how the elements of the communications plan actually drove the final outcome. Of course, we know that many factors out of the planner's control significantly affect sales—pricing, the product, distribution and competitive factors, not to mention the creative work. But in this era of Google advertising precision and accountability, it's not enough to say "Media's done its job, we achieved the ratings or delivered the advertising to the right audience."

In this new media world of marketing science and communications accountability there has to be a willingness for higher responsibility to know what worked. We need to be able to answer the hard questions. There has to be a stronger work ethic behind learning how to improve and optimize plan performance. And I aim to show you how to achieve that with this chapter.

THE NUMBERS TELL THE STORY

I'm a huge fan of professional basketball. I love the athleticism and skill of a LeBron James dunk and the drama and anticipation that builds when the coach calls a time-out for the final play of the game with just seconds left on the clock. It's pure magic. But what really fascinates me is viewing TNT's *T-Mobile Half Time Show*, where the TV commentators pore over the stats to explain how the game has unfolded and what each team needs to do to win the game.

Former All Star player and television analyst Charles Barkley will comment, "The Celtics have forced six turnovers in the first half; Miami needs to look after the basketball if they are to get back into this game." Former Rockets player Kenny Smith will observe, "The difference between Houston and Dallas tonight is the outside shooting. Houston is shooting 64 percent versus Dallas 23 percent. The Mavs are going to have to defend the Rockets more aggressively and look for easier shots inside the paint."

Similarly, it's the marketing statistics that tell the nonstop, ever evolving action in advertising. More importantly, they give very good direction as to how to win the Brand Media Strategy game. Just like sports coaches, a communications planner needs a strategy to win, and that involves making the adjustments needed to improve the outcome.

ADVERTISING CAUSE AND EFFECT JUST GOT HARDER

Proving advertising cause and effect has become a much more challenging issue in today's digital media world. On the one hand, everything is more measurable, but on the other hand, according to Frank Harrison, ZenithOptimedia's worldwide director of strategic resources, "In just a few years, the volume of influences on consumer purchase decisions has grown hugely, both those within and outside of the brand managers' control."[2]

Media's long tail is making it more difficult to be as effective, fragmentation is splitting the audience, and consumers are subject to a much more complex decision-making process. All have an effect on the business and marketing environment. It is harder today to understand what works and what doesn't. "In US companies, both large and small, the goal of achieving true, demonstrable accountability for the marketing function, if it is considered at all, is one that has proven elusive for years."[3] And while companies' senior management and finance departments are demanding that marketing provide them with a higher level of accountability, only 14 percent of senior marketers felt confident in forecasts of how marketing activities would affect sales.[4]

METRICS MUST BE DRIVEN BY OBJECTIVES AND TARGETS

Research is big business in the United States, where around $8.6 billion is spent trying to figure out consumption and media habits.[5]

The problem in media isn't that we don't have enough data; it's that there is too much. The communications industry, particularly the part that deals with measuring media, is overloaded with metrics. There are tracking studies, competitive reporting, consumer segmentation, product usage and attitudinal studies, media currencies, online surveys, copy testing and econometric modeling, in addition to literally billions of data points now being collected in digital media.

There are numerous audience surveys for each medium. Television alone is tracked by Nielsen, TiVo, Rentrak and Kantar Media, among many others. Pay-television companies are researching set-top boxes that could offer precision targeting from individual household data. And the recession has accentuated the desire to add to this data pile. It's easy to lose track or be overwhelmed.

In some cases research is used simply to justify the job. Many times its proof of measurability is used as a surrogate for accountability. Of course there is a need to measure success, but research should be about influencing decision making. The trick is reading and tracking only the data that helps make better decisions.

The role of research is twofold: steer and track the strategy, and develop and optimize the tactics.

STEER AND TRACK THE BRAND MEDIA STRATEGY

Before surrounding yourself with data and research, start with a definition of what success looks like. Chapter 4, "Focusing on Outcomes, Not Outputs," deals with this in great detail. Marketers want to see how the Brand Media Strategy is driving clear outcomes and communications effectiveness.

As pointed out in chapter 4, communication goals need to be established at the outset. They need to align with appropriate stages of the Consumer Pathway and demonstrate a clear line of sight to how the communications will influence the business outcome. The key performance indicators (KPIs) should quantify the communication goals and help determine what and how effective the Brand Media Strategy is.

Focus on a few metrics, ideally just the most significant one. KPIs should measure the collective impact of media and message. Measurement should not try to determine media's success separate from creative's. Both need to work to drive the overall communications. Nor is it about measuring the individual effectiveness of each medium. The communications planner drives the holistic impact of the entire plan.

One of Optimedia's retail-based client's goals was centered on driving acquisition. Their brand awareness levels weren't high, but we assessed that brand consideration was the core issue. Only one in five switchers would consider the brand. We measured individual components of the client's media program, but the overriding focus was on shifting consideration. We made significant adjustments in the media mix and the messaging. Budget was shifted into newspapers and magazines, while the client honed their online program toward consideration-based offers. Traditional measures of coverage and efficiency actually fell slightly, but consideration increased by nearly 50 percent, and acquisitions improved.

The Consumer Pathway provides the foundation for setting the communication goals and establishing the KPIs, used to evaluate a communications campaign. The KPIs for each stage of the Consumer Pathway warrant different strategies and tactics and different measurement. Some example KPIs are shown in figure 12.1.

Marketing research departments tend to measure all the different stages of the Consumer Pathway, but focusing on one or two KPIs will deliver a more focused communications effort and increase the likelihood of success. The best campaigns, I've noticed, come with a clear and single-minded goal and metric.

THE CAMPAIGN MEASUREMENT PROCESS

DETERMINE OBJECTIVES AND SUCCESS CRITERIA

The purpose here is to define the quantifiable goal along the Consumer Pathway, either one or a combination of the following: awareness, involvement, active consideration and intent, trial, purchase, loyalty and advocacy. Specify explicit success targets for the goals (for example, increase product awareness X percent from the current level).

FIGURE 12.1

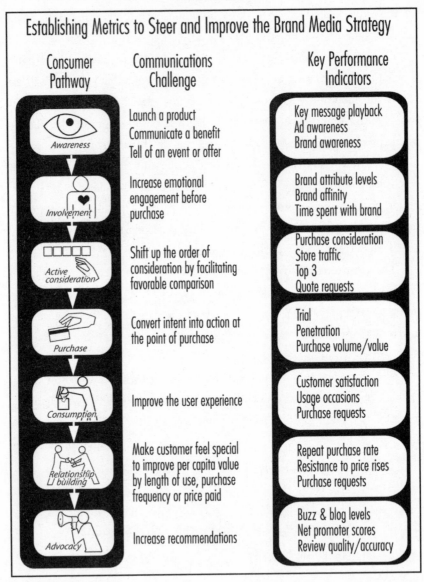

Establishing Metrics to Steer and Improve the Brand Media Strategy

Consumer Pathway	Communications Challenge	Key Performance Indicators
Awareness	Launch a product Communicate a benefit Tell of an event or offer	Key message playback Ad awareness Brand awareness
Involvement	Increase emotional engagement before purchase	Brand attribute levels Brand affinity Time spent with brand
Active consideration	Shift up the order of consideration by facilitating favorable comparison	Purchase consideration Store traffic Top 3 Quote requests
Purchase	Convert intent into action at the point of purchase	Trial Penetration Purchase volume/value
Consumption	Improve the user experience	Customer satisfaction Usage occasions Purchase requests
Relationship building	Make customer feel special to improve per capita value by length of use, purchase frequency or price paid	Repeat purchase rate Resistance to price rises Purchase requests
Advocacy	Increase recommendations	Buzz & blog levels Net promoter scores Review quality/accuracy

For the Denny's Super Bowl Grand Slam Giveaway, our communication goal was to get people to come back to Denny's one more time. The KPI was guest-count traffic.

IDENTIFY LEARNING OBJECTIVES AND ANALYSIS APPROACH

Measurement is an ongoing process of building knowledge and experience to aid future planning.

Three months before the Denny's Super Bowl promotion, we had tested different media tactics with the client. We tested two key variables: First, we targeted what we called the "breakfast super fan," as opposed to the more general target. Second, the client bought television ad time in college football play-off games leading into the holiday season. We saw positive increases in guest counts when this activity was coordinated with an offer.

IDENTIFY METRICS AND DATA SOURCES

Marrying the metrics to the goals and tactics involves identifying metrics and data sources. I suggest breaking metrics into two groups: tracking, to gauge response, and diagnostics, to determine improvement opportunities. Then identify data sources and reporting requirements to implement measurement tracking.

We had several business metrics for Denny's, such as guest counts on the promotion day and for the six weeks after the Grand Slam giveaway promotion. The client set the expectation of a positive marketing ROI for these periods. Secondary communication goals included visits to the website and, in particular, using the restaurant locator function on the website. We tracked the audience reach of the Super Bowl spot and the cost effectiveness of the buy relative to other advertisers, and we tracked the favorability of the commercial itself to the audience.

DEFINE MEASUREMENT AND REPORTING PLAN

Eventually, there is a requirement to build a consolidated measurement plan outlining objectives, metrics, methodology, data infrastructure, test design and recommended reporting and the analysis schedule. If applicable, this could also include measurement tool assessment.

In addition to the business metrics, we included all media data sources that tracked the Denny's promotion: television audience ratings and reach, buzz via Search, Twitter and blogs, and established targets for paid search.

COMMUNICATE MEASUREMENT PLAN

Communicate guidelines of data reporting requirements to all necessary stakeholders.

For Denny's media reach, estimates were established up front so as to get approval of the plan. Measurement reporting such as overnight ratings and online metrics were sent to senior executives the day after the Super Bowl spot ran.

COLLECT DATA, INTERPRET AND ANALYZE RESULTS

Be descriptive: what is happening? Be diagnostic: why is it happening? Ask: how can we improve performance?

When the Denny's campaign launched, we saw a huge number of news stories about the campaign. We measured the reach and value of the PR in addition to the media campaign itself. When the campaign ended, the team analyzed the results and saw an opportunity to extend it beyond the six-week run of the promotion by building a database for future campaigns to extend and remarket to customers.

MARKETING AND PROCESS OPTIMIZATION

Create and reestablish baseline and benchmark metrics. Refine the marketing strategy and redefine learning priorities. After year one, we had the data and experience of the previous year's campaign and were then able to set more specific target and ROI goals for year two.

Figure 12.2 illustrates the process.

FIGURE 12.2

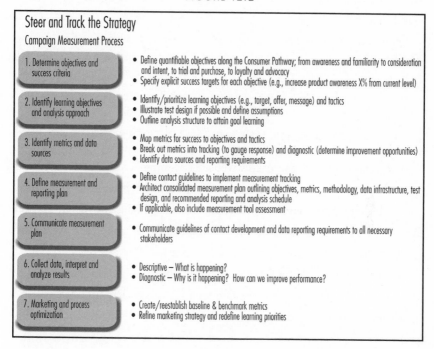

Steer and Track the Strategy
Campaign Measurement Process

1. Determine objectives and success criteria
- Define quantifiable objectives along the Consumer Pathway; from awareness and familiarity to consideration and intent, to trial and purchase, to loyalty and advocacy
- Specify explicit success targets for each objective (e.g., increase product awareness X% from current level)

2. Identify learning objectives and analysis approach
- Identify/prioritize learning objectives (e.g., target, offer, message) and tactics
- Illustrate test design if possible and define assumptions
- Outline analysis structure to attain goal learning

3. Identify metrics and data sources
- Map metrics for success to objectives and tactics
- Break out metrics into tracking (to gauge response) and diagnostic (determine improvement opportunities)
- Identify data sources and reporting requirements

4. Define measurement and reporting plan
- Define contact guidelines to implement measurement tracking
- Architect consolidated measurement plan outlining objectives, metrics, methodology, data infrastructure, test design, and recommended reporting and analysis schedule
- If applicable, also include measurement tool assessment

5. Communicate measurement plan
- Communicate guidelines of contact development and data reporting requirements to all necessary stakeholders

6. Collect data, interpret and analyze results
- Descriptive – What is happening?
- Diagnostic – Why is it happening? How can we improve performance?

7. Marketing and process optimization
- Create/reestablish baseline & benchmark metrics
- Refine marketing strategy and redefine learning priorities

USING ONLINE DATA TO TRACK CAMPAIGN PERFORMANCE

Probably one of the most efficient ways to collect campaign data is through online measurement. I've found that online data is useful for more than measuring online campaigns or evaluating direct response campaigns. While not a replacement for brand or sales tracking, online metrics can indicate how the entire media communications effort is performing.

If the communications goal is to drive active consideration, then measuring who is visiting the branded website and what they do once they get there yields valuable insight. For example, are they requesting more information or downloading content? If the goal is to raise awareness for a product or service, as is the case in much pharmaceutical consumer-based advertising, it can be measured by how often the drug or generic medical condition is searched for. If the goal is to drive advocacy, measuring blogs, tweets, conversations, postings and product reviews is a useful method to gauge impact.

While these by no means offer boardroom-proof evidence of marketing ROI, they can provide planners real-time and dynamic indicators of consumer response to a campaign.

ONLINE MEASUREMENT TOOLS

Google Analytics and the brand website's webmaster can provide sound data on search inquiries and traffic and behavior. Many online tools measure and quantify the level of blogs, posts, social media conversations and Tweets. Most of them are free. Here is a selection of some that I've found useful.

Google Insights: With Google Insights for search, you can compare search volume patterns across specific regions, categories, time frames and properties. It provides the most commonly searched keywords around a term as well as keywords rising in search popularity.

HowSociable: HowSociable measures brand visibility across the social web. It tracks a brand across thirty-two social media metrics and provides a visibility that can be used to compare one brand to another.

Social Mention: Social Mention is a social media search platform that aggregates user-generated content from across the internet into a single stream of information. It allows you to easily track what people are saying about you, your company, a new product or any topic across the web's social media landscape in real time.

Twitalyzer: Twitalyzer is a cool site that evaluates the activity of any brand in Twitter and reports on relative strength, signal-to-noise ratio, favor, passion, clout and other useful measures of success in social media.

Twitrratr: With Twitrratr you can distinguish negative from positive tweets surrounding a brand, product, person or topic. Twitter search results are cross-referenced against positive and negative keyword lists and the results are displayed accordingly.

Wordle: Wordle is a program for generating "word clouds" from text that you provide. The clouds give greater prominence to words that appear more frequently in the source text. You can tweak your clouds with different fonts, layouts and color schemes.

AWARENESS, WHAT SORT OF AWARENESS?

Speaking at the Measure Up conference I attended in March 2010, Kevin Clancy, chief executive officer of Copernicus Marketing Consultancy, said there are twenty-five different awareness metrics that range from unaided advertising to specific message registration.[6] The skill is determining which awareness level to focus on, which are related to the category or the communication goal.

One test is to ask the consumer to name the first brand that comes to mind when mentioning a particular category (top-of-mind awareness). It is generally a good barometer for brand preference and market share. Another test is that of unaided advertising awareness. Clancy claims that general awareness is about twice the brand's share of voice, and it is partially related to the volume of advertising but has more to do with how established the brand is. Then there is also specific advertising message awareness, which involves asking, "Have you seen or heard any advertising for XXX in the past thirty days that uses the slogan 'YYY'?" This measurement is highly sensitive to changes in advertising.

MARKET-MIX MODELING

Essentially, market-mix, or econometric, modeling isolates individual marketing or media variables to determine their effect on sales. Companies such as Procter & Gamble, Johnson & Johnson and Reckitt Benckiser are strong advocates of this work, and many advertisers in financial services, telecoms and retail regularly undertake analytics. It's used to help direct media mixes and used to measure ROI. For example, with television it can help brands identify the best times of day, channels, days of the week, spot lengths and effectiveness of different creative.

From a planning perspective, market-mix modeling is the gold standard as it evaluates the effectiveness and efficiency of media options based on a true return on investment. However, it is costly to implement and so for many clients is not an option.

ALL THE SCIENCE CANNOT REPLACE HUMANS

Econometric modeling only improves what you have done in the past. It relies on data collected over numerous past campaigns. So if you've only ever advertised on television, it won't provide data on other media. For companies like Reckitt Benckiser, which know that television is the principal driver of repeat sales, that's not an issue. However, if there is a need for change in a brand or marketing strategy, or a new product or category is being launched, then it is less helpful.

Econometric modeling can measure only short-term impacts on sales. This form of tracking works efficiently for fast-moving consumer goods or retailers. It's more difficult to use for big-ticket items or highly involved purchases such as automobiles, for business products or in major brand efforts to change perceptions.

As marketers require more certainty and measurability in their strategies, modeling techniques are improving.

DEVELOP AND OPTIMIZE THE TACTICS

Planners have numerous metrics to deploy to develop and fine-tune the media plan. And just as in the basketball analogy, tracking individual player statistics can help them improve their game.

These metrics are important for improving the quality of selection and optimizing the efficiency of the media budget. They provide comparisons for planning trade-offs and making buying decisions.

MEDIA PLANNING CURRENCIES

Media planning currencies include impressions, gross rating points, reach and frequency, page views and unique views, to name a few. They are used to report the size of the audience exposed via media panels.

Each medium is measured differently. Print readership is measured through independently verified surveys; television and radio audiences are determined by people meters or diaries; out-of-home audiences are tracked through traffic surveys. Complicating it all are the different definitions of what constitutes an impression in each media category.

Media currencies are used to quantify and support the media planning of campaigns and negotiate trading terms with media based on the size of the audience. They track individual media vehicles to help make decisions on station, title or site selection and various positions to secure.

REACH AND FREQUENCY

Reach quantifies the coverage of the target audience a medium delivers. Usually, it only measures a single medium's reach, but agencies have developed models to estimate the combined coverage of multiple media types.

Frequency determines the intensity of the advertising. The higher the frequency, the more persuasive and more visible the campaign is.

SHARE OF VOICE

In marketing there is a common assumption that high share of voice is an important measure of media competitiveness. According to Ipsos ASI, which tracks marketing performance via its Brand*Graph database, share of voice has a positive correlation with advertising recall and impact.[7] However, this correlation is less influential in driving recall than other factors such as creative quality, high reach, scheduling of advertising and avoiding wear-out of creative.

The impact of advertising creative is often more important than share of voice, so the communications planner needs to consider this in the planning process. Investing in strong copy is an important consideration. The planner needs to ask how strong the creative is and, in particular, how it meets the brand objectives.

Reach, frequency and share of voice are measures that quantify the scale of media presence but lack an evaluative assessment of receptivity or attention to the communications. They are estimates of potential exposures or impressions but not the "depth" of impressions. Planning in media is a bit like buying fish at a fish market. You weigh the fish but also check its quality, hence the growing development of engagement metrics.

ENGAGEMENT METRICS

Planners interested in increasing communications influence and involvement are studying engagement metrics. However, *engagement* isn't universally defined; there is no standard currency despite many attempts to measure it.

The Advertising Research Foundation employed a task force that found over fifty different research studies and methodologies that measured media engagement.[8] Studies measure time spent viewing particular media, brainwave activity in response to stimuli and impact of media environments on advertising recall and purchase intent. Often these are sponsored by individual media owners, pushing the merits of their medium. Of course, the sponsors of such studies have an agenda, but I try to keep an open mind. If a media company has deeper insights into their particular consumer, then a study they sponsor is worth considering.

Nielsen IAG aims to quantify how closely viewers are paying attention to television shows and commercials. It surveys a panel of television viewers each night on how well they recall the details of programs, sponsorships, branded integrations, product placements and ads they've seen in the past twenty-four hours. Nielsen IAG co–chief executive officer Alan Gould claims the service helps advertisers "make smarter decisions" about which programs and ads are performing best. "We'll see advertisers buying TV spots increasingly on the basis of how engaged the audience is, not just how big it is," he says.[9]

METRICS IN YOUR FUTURE

Little advancement in media can take place without commonly agreed upon measurement standards. The business models of tomorrow are being decided in meetings today.

The world of television product placement and integration did not take off en masse until Nielsen acquired IAG and began to provide marketers with metrics to help evaluate what is seen and discussed on-screen. The global recession brought renewed vigor for addressable advertising advancements, which aim to deliver customized targeted television ads to individual households on the basis of profile data, for example, the proverbial cat food ads to cat owners. Such developments are set to reinvent the media landscape for marketers who want greater precision in directing ad dollars at their target.

Cable and satellite companies are moving closer to delivering the scale necessary for marketers to give them a second look. The two biggest satellite providers in the market, DirecTV and Dish, are now working together to provide interactive television channels that allow the consumer to pull down more information on products advertised through requests for information.

Google, Facebook and Twitter want users to disclose their location so Madison Avenue can at the very least serve up ads to those in a specific geographic market. Once mobile video advertising becomes more measurable, targeting by simple geography will seem old hat.

Meanwhile, Google continues its march into the television advertising business with its support of new tech companies such as Invidi, which slices and dices audiences to deliver more precise ad messages.

What's clear is that measurement for the communications planner takes on greater proportions as technology facilitates gathering more and better access to data and as marketers evince increased interest in greater visibility of ROI. The planner needs to keep in mind that measurement isn't about reporting and justification. It is about making better decisions and adjustments that steer the strategy and tactics.

QUESTIONS ON INCORPORATING
METRICS AND MEASUREMENT

1. Are the KPIs aligned to the communication goals?
2. What are the one or two most important metrics for this campaign?
3. Do we have established benchmarks to set meaningful goals?
4. How can the data help me steer or change the plan?

FURTHER READING

Kellogg on Advertising and Media
Bobby Calder and Philip Kotler
Wiley, 2008

How Disruption Brought Order: The Story of a Winning Strategy in the World of Advertising
Jean-Marie Dru
Palgrave Macmillan, 2007

From Prime Time to My Time—Audience Measurement in the Digital Age
Andrew Green
WARC, 2010

Made to Stick: Why Some Ideas Survive and Others Die
Chip Heath and Dan Heath
Random House, 2007

The Global Brand
Nigel Hollis
Palgrave Macmillan, 2008

How Advertising Works: The Role of Research
John Philip Jones
Sage, 1998

Virtual Worlds: Rewiring Your Emotional Future
Jack Myers
Myers Publishing, 2007

Microtrends: The Small Forces behind Tomorrow's Big Changes
Mark Penn and E. Kinney Zalesne
Twelve, 2009

The Online Advertising Playbook: Proven Strategies and Tested Tactics from the Advertising Research Foundation
Joe Plummer, Steve Rappaport, Taddy Hall and Robert Barocci
Wiley, 2007

Lovemarks
Kevin Roberts
Powerhouse Books, 2004

Space Race: An Inside View of the Future of Communications Planning
Jim Taylor
Wiley, 2005

Profitable Marketing Communications: A Guide to Marketing Return on Investment
Antony Young and Lucy Aitken
Kogan Page, 2007

NOTES

INTRODUCTION

1. ZenithOptimedia Worldwide Advertising Spending Forecasts, April 2010.

CHAPTER 1: GOOGLE AND FACEBOOK

1. ComScore and Kelsey Group, "Online consumer-generated reviews have significant impact on offline purchase behavior," News release, November 29, 2007, www.comscore.com/Press _Events/Press_Releases/.
2. Kenneth Hein, "Teen Talk Is, Like, Totally Branded," *Brandweek,* August 6, 2007, http://www.brandweek.com/bw/esearch/article_display.jsp?vnu_content_id=1003621840.
3. John Battelle, *The Search: How Google and Its Rivals Rewrote the Rules of Business and Transformed Our Culture* (New York: Penguin, Portfolio, 2005), 4.
4. David A. Vise and Mark Malseed, *The Google Story* (New York: Bantam Dell, 2005), 118.
5. Paul Bond Sr., interview by Maria Bartiromo, "Inside the Mind of Google," *Original,* CNBC, December 3, 2009.
6. Ken Auletta, *Googled: The End of the World as We Know It* (Boston: Penguin, 2009).
7. "comScore Reports Global Search Market Growth of 46 Percent in 2009," ComScore, http://www.comscore.com/Press_Events/Press_Releases/2010/1/Global_Search_Market_Grows _46_Percent_in_2009.
8. Eric Schmidt, CEO Google Inc. (speaking at Atmosphere, Google's conference for chief information officers, Mountain View, CA, April 12, 2010).
9. Heather Dougherty, Director, Research at Hitwise, "Facebook Reaches Top Ranking in US," Hitwise.com, March 15, 2010.
10. Garry Pierre-Pierre, "Social networks keep Haitian people informed and comforted," *Haitian Times,* January 19, 2010.
11. Kirkpatrick, *The Facebook Effect: The Inside Story of the Company That Is Connecting the World* (New York: Simon & Schuster, 2010), 210.
12. Brian Morrissey, "Success Factors for Brands on Facebook," Adweek.com, October 12, 2009.
13. Facebook.com/cocacola, July 17, 2010.
14. Facebook.com/starbucks, July 17, 2010.

CHAPTER 2: THE NEW MEDIA PLAYBOOK

1. "Nike Inc." Encyclopedia Britannica, EB.com.
2. Louise Story, "The New Advertising Outlet: Your Life," *New York Times,* October 14, 2007.
3. "Video: NIKE's classic 'Ronaldinho: Touch of Gold'—(over 28 million views on YouTube)," www.BallHype.com, April 18, 2009, http://ballhype.com/video/video_nike_classic_ronald inho_touch_of_gold_over_28/.
4. Hidalgo, "Nike Marketing: Letting the Consumer Decide," (Association of National Advertisers' Masters of Marketing conference, Orlando, FL, October 13, 2008).

5.   Chris Anderson, *The Long Tail: Why the Future of Business Is Selling Less of More* (New York: Hyperion, 2006).
6.   Olek, "The World Cup Brand Winner: Adidas or Nike?" HBR.org, July 9, 2010.
7.   Louise Story, "The New Advertising Outlet: Your Life," *New York Times*, October 14, 2007.
8.   "BIGresearch Releases 11th Simultaneous Media Survey: More People Multitasking Media Than Ever; Videos on Cell Phones Fastest Growing New Media, Web Radio Grows, TV's Influence to Purchase Declines," Internet Wire, January 22, 2008.
9.   Nielsen TV Audience Measurement, Nielsen Company, qtd. in "TV Ratings: 1986–1987," ClassicTVHits.com, http://www.classictvhits.com/tvratings/1985.htm.
10. Three Screen Report, Q1 2010, Nielsen Company.
11. David C. Court, Jonathon W. Gordon, and Jesko Perrey, "Boosting returns on marketing investment," *McKinsey Quarterly* no. 2, 2005.
12. "Synovate In:fact global study on media and advertising," conducted in September 2009, surveying 8,600 respondents across 11 markets—Australia, Brazil, Canada, China, Hong Kong, India, the Netherlands, Spain, Taiwan, the UK and the US, www.synovate.com.
13. Christopher Heine, "WPP to Leverage Kantar Data for Media Planning," *ClickZ*, December 15, 2009.
14. Ragnhild Kjetland, "Playboy Surfers Targeted for VW Polos in Web Video Ads," *Bloomberg*, February 5, 2010.
15. Ibid.
16. Ibid.
17. Survey by Cision and Don Bates of the George Washington University Graduate School of Political Management. Sent to 9,100 editors/journalists in the fall of 2009, published January 20, 2010.
18. *Shop: How Shoppers Decide*, Netpop Research, February 2008.
19. Report prepared by Carleen Hawn, Susanna Hamner and Erick Schonfeld, *How to Succeed in 2007*, Business 2.0 Magazine, February 28, 2007.
20. "Fifth ANA/Forrester Survey Measures Marketers' Attitudes toward TV/Video Advertising," Association of National Advertisers and Forrester Research, February 8, 2010.
21. Donaton, *Madison and Vine* (New York: McGraw-Hill, 2005).
22. Lev Grossman, "Time's Person of the Year: You," *Time*, December 13, 2006.
23. Reported by Steve McClellan, "SMG, Comcast: Addressable System Cuts Ad Skipping," *Adweek*, February 19, 2010.

CHAPTER 3: A SHIFT FROM MEDIA PLANNING TO COMMUNICATIONS PLANNING

1.   Steven J. Heyer, Keynote remarks as COO, Coca-Cola Co. (Advertising Age's Madison + Vine conference, Beverly Hills Hotel, Beverly Hills, CA, February 5, 2003).
2.   Taylor, *Space Race* (Chichester, West Sussex, England: Wiley, 2005), 4.
3.   Matthew Creamer, "Bring Out the Account Planners," *Advertising Age*, April 17, 2006.
4.   Michael E. Porter, "What Is Strategy?" *HBROnPoint*, February 2000.
5.   "Marketers Strive to Become Visionaries, yet ANA/Prophet Study Indicates Most Perform at Tactical Levels," *State of Marketing Survey: The Shift*, ANA/Prophet, November 10, 2009, http://www.ana.net/news/content/1969.

CHAPTER 4: FOCUSING ON OUTCOMES, NOT OUTPUTS

1.   Jennifer Rooney, "CMO's Stuck Around Even Longer in '08," *Advertising Age*, January 30, 2009.
2.   "Marketing Execs Struggle to Show ROI," The Conference Board, http://www.marketingcharts.com/interactive/marketing-execs-struggle-to-show-roi–7634/.
3.   Antony Young and Lucy Aitken, *Profitable Marketing Communications* (London: Kogan Page, 2007).
4.   Marchese, "Why Advertise at All?" *Mediapost*, June 30, 2009.

5.   "The End of Marketing as We Know It," Zyman Group, LLC, http://www.zyman.com/ourThinking_institute.asp.

6.   John Philip Jones, *How Advertising Works* (Thousand Oaks, CA: Sage, 1998).

7.   Young and Aitken, 72–74.

8.   Quinn, "Customer Centric Marketing," (ANA Masters of Marketing Annual Conference, Phoenix, Arizona, November 6, 2009).

CHAPTER 5: INSIGHT OVER ANALYSIS

1.   First attributed to Cliff Stoll and Gary Schubert, in Mark R. Keeler, *Nothing to Hide: Privacy in the 21st Century* (Lincoln, NE: iUniverse Inc., 2006), 112.

2.   Jon Steel, *Truth, Lies and Advertising: The Art of Account Planning* (New York: John Wiley & Sons, Inc., 1998), 36.

3.   Peter Francese, "America 2010: What the 2010 Census Means for Marketers and Advertiser," *Advertising Age*, October 11, 2009.

4.   Bradley Johnson, "New U.S. Census to Reveal Major Shift: No More Joe Consumer" *Advertising Age*, October 12, 2009.

5.   Mark Penn and E. Kinney Zalesne, *Microtrends: The Small Forces behind Tomorrow's Big Changes* (New York: Twelve, 2009).

6.   Nintendo, "Wii Would Like to Play." Gold winner, New Product, Effie Awards 2008, http://www.effie.org/winners/showcase/2008/2331.

7.   "A Conversation with Mark Penn," www.microtrending.com/conversation.php.

8.   "Steve Jobs: There's Sanity Returning," *BusinessWeek*, May 25, 1998.

9.   Michael Harvey, "Will Client Insight Functions Survive the Recession?" *Market Leader*, October 2009, 54–55.

10. Tom Neveril, CMO Strategy, "Behavior Defines Consumers," *Advertising Age*, July 16, 2007.

11. Chuck Salter, "Can Hulu Save Traditional TV?" *Fast Company*, November 2009.

12. Advokator, "What We Do: Discovery," http://www.quocom.biz/adv-wwd.htm.

13. Jack Neff, "ARF: Consumer Opinions Online Still Seen as Curse, Not Gift," *Advertising Age*, January 11, 2010.

14. MTV 2010/2011 Upfront presentation (Hammerstein Ballroom, New York City, February 2, 2010).

15. Catalina Marketing's Pointer Media Network and the CMO Council, *Discovering the Pivotal Point Consumer*, December 2008.

CHAPTER 6: 1 + 1 = 3

1.   TREMOR website, "Why does consumer advocacy drive your business?" http://www.tremor.com/driving-business-with-consumer-advocacy/why-does-consumer-advocacy-drive-your-business/.

2.   Godin, *Meatball Sundae: Is Your Marketing Out of Sync?* (New York: Penguin, Portfolio, 2008), 79.

3.   Frank Rose, "Let the Seller Beware," *Wall Street Journal*, December 20, 2006.

4.   Godin, 119.

5.   Keller Fay Group, TalkTrack survey, August 2007–September 2008.

6.   Keller, Measure Up Conference (Conrad Hilton, Chicago, March 12, 2010).

7.   Fay, Cakim, Carpenter, Hershberger, O'Driscoll, Rabasca, Selvas and Suckernek *WOMMA Influencer Handbook: The Who, What, When, Where, How and Why of Influencer Marketing* (Chicago: WOMMA, December 2008).

8.   Gladwell, *The Tipping Point* (Boston: Back Bay Books, 2002), 61.

9.   ICOM, a division of Epsilon Targeting, Influencer study 2007–2009, released March 2010.

10. Rogers, *Diffusion of Innovations,* (New York: Free Press, 2003) 5th ed.

11. Rich, "Shiny New Things: What Digital Adopters Want, How to Reach Them, and Why Every Marketer Should Pay Attention," Advertising Age White Paper, March 15, 2010, 5.

12. Ibid.

13. Bough, "Social Analysis—Real-Time Insights for Your Brand," Ad:Tech, New York, November 5, 2009.
14. Ibid.
15. Ibid.
16. Tylee, "How Brands Are Making Conversations," *Campaign,* February 26, 2010.
17. North America Technographics Media & Marketing online survey Q2, 2008. Forrester Research, December 3, 2008.
18. Zyman, *The End of Advertising as We Know It* (Hoboken, NJ: Wiley, 2002), 9.
19. Hein, "Incentive Marketing: Employees can help to make or break a new campaign, so why not market to them first?" *Brandweek,* February 16, 2009.
20. Ryan, Method's "Method for Green Growth," Association of National Advertisers, Masters of Marketing Conference, November 7, 2009.
21. "The Dark Night," http://boxofficemojo.com/movies/?id=darkknight.htm.
22. Maymann, "The Dark Knight Batman movie and attention planning for viral campaigns," Warc Exclusive, October 2008.
23. Foster Farms' "Say No to Plumping," New York American Marketing Association, Gold, North America Effies 2010, Goodby, Silverstein, & Partners, http://www.effie.org/winners/showcase/2010/4344.
24. Ibid.; Juliana Barbassa, "Chicken producers debate whether poultry injected with salt, water should qualify as 'natural,'" *Washington Examiner,* July 30, 2010, http://www.washington examiner.com/breaking/chicken-producers-debate-natural-label-99609209.html#ixzz0vyjFu M00.
25. Case provided to the author by Publicis Worldwide.
26. Pepsi Refresh Project, http://www.refresheverything.com.
27. James, "American Idols: YouTube and other media trends from some of the 2008 US Effie winners," WARC online, September 2008.
28. Ibid.
29. JetBlue Airways "Amplification" 2007 Effie Award Winner, http://www.effie.org/winners/showcase/2007/1617, 2007.
30. Keller, "Super Bowl Sunday—What Drives Word of Mouth Success for Advertisers?" Media bizbloggers.com, February 3, 2010, http://www.jackmyers.com/commentary/media-business-bloggers/83378382.html.

CHAPTER 7: CONDUCTING THE ORCHESTRA

1. Association of National Advertisers, "Integrated Marketing Study" (New York: 2008).
2. Advertising Works 17, IPA Effectiveness Awards (London: WARC, March 2009).
3. "Pepsi—Wake Up People," Effie Worldwide, New York, Beverages—Non-Alcohol, Effie Awards 2008, http://www.effie.org/winners/showcase/2008/2643.
4. Mediacom UK, Partners in Indulgence, Mars UK, http://www.creamglobal.com/search/17798/16963/partners-in-indulgence/.
5. Geoffrey Precourt, "21st Century Integration: From Theory to Practice" (WARC, August 2009).
6. Golding, "Losing It All," *Campaign,* Integration Essays, December 3, 2009.
7. Ritson, "The industry's ideal handyman is proving to be an elusive entity," *Marketing,* November 21, 2002.

CHAPTER 8: UNLOCKING MOMENTS OF RECEPTIVITY

1. Abbey Klaassen, "Stop with the Engagement Already, It's about Receptivity," *Advertising Age,* November 29, 2006.
2. Graciela Eleta, "The Transformation of America: Playing to Win in a Multicultural Nation" (Focus Group comments included in the presentation, 4A Transformation conference, San Francisco, March 2, 2010).
3. Citroen C5, OMD UK, Case Study, http://www.ipa.co.uk/Content/TouchPoints-Site-Citroen-C5-OMD-UK-Case-Study.

4.   IAB UK survey conducted by Lightspeed Research's UK online panel between 28 November and 8 December 2008.
5.   US Army Xbox Halo 3 (New York American Marketing Association, Brand Experience, Effie Awards 2009).
6.   Elaine Wong, "Ikea Builds Own Oval Office for Obama," *Brandweek,* January 12, 2009.
7.   Emily Nussbaum, "What Tina Fey Would Do for a SoyJoy," *New York Magazine,* October 5, 2008.
8.   Ausiello, "ABC plots groundbreaking 'Housewives' spin-off," EW.com, September 7, 2009.
9.   "Orange Gold Spots—Don't Let a Mobile Phone Ruin Your Movie," Account Planning Group (UK), Creative Strategy Awards, 2009.
10. Ryan Gilbey, "Orange's cinematic ads that are actually worth watching," *The Guardian,* April 6, 2009, http://www.guardian.co.uk/film/filmblog/2009/apr/06/orange-film-board-adverts.
11. B. Sheehan and A. Young, "Convergence, Contradiction and Collaboration," in *Handbook of Research on Digital Media and Advertising: User Generated Content Consumption,* ed. Matthew S. Eastin, Terry Daugherty and Neal M. Burns (Austin, TX: IGI Global, 2010), 275–299.

CHAPTER 9: TOUCH-POINT SELECTION

1.   Bain/IAB 2009 Marketer survey; Bain Media 3.0 Study, 2009, included in a presentation to IAB members, "Building Brands Online: An Interactive Advertising Action Plan," November 12, 2009.
2.   Kamp, Boon and Bruin, "Sara Lee International Case Study," Cross Media Effectiveness Research—ESOMAR Best Research Paper Award, June 2005.
3.   Personal conversation with the author.
4.   New York American Marketing Association, Gold, Delivery Products and Services, The Martin Agency, Effie Awards 2008.

CHAPTER 10: DIGITIZING THE BRAND MEDIA STRATEGY

1.   ZenithOptimedia, Worldwide Advertising Spending Forecasts, July 2010.
2.   Laura Martin, "Advertising Wars—Who Wins?" *Needham Insights,* Needham & Company, April 6, 2010.
3.   Twitter.com as of July 5, 2010.
4.   Hayzlett conversation with author, May 17, 2010.
5.   Skcin—computertan.com, Account Planning Group (UK) Creative Strategy Awards, 2009.
6.   Ibid.
7.   Brunelli, "The AdWeek Media Plan of the Year 2009," *Adweek,* June 14, 2009.
8.   Ibid.
9.   *Cream,* http://peoplesaward.creamglobal.com/casestudy.cfm?i=67.
10. Nielsen, "Three Screen Report," Fourth quarter, 2009.
11. iProspect Offline Channel Influence on Online Search Behavior Study, August 2007.
12. Presentation by Angela O'Connell, head of cross-media research at Google Europe, and Lucas Hulsebos, media research director at MetrixLab, Re:think 2009, The 55th annual convention of the Advertising Research Foundation (New York, March 30–April 1, 2009).
13. Report titled "SEO vs. PPC—The Final Round" by Engine Ready of a study undertaken between July 1, 2008, through June 30, 2009.
14. Brian Quinton, "Should You Buy Your Brand?" *Direct,* Nov. 30, 2006, http://multichannelmerchant.com/ecommerce/buy_your-brand_11302006/index.html.
15. T. L. Stanley, "Edelman: PR Agency of the Year '09," *Adweek,* Feb. 22, 2010.
16. Bob Greenberg, "A Platform for Life," *Adweek,* September 14, 2009.
17. The Visa Business Network, http://www.visabusinessnetwork.com/networking/feature_me#.
18. Ellie Parpis, "Marketer of the Year '09: David Plouffe," *Brandweek,* September 14, 2009.
19. Ibid.
20. Young, "Hillary vs. Barack: Who Had the Smartest Media Strategy?" *Advertising Age,* June 4, 2008.
21. Jennifer Fermino, "'Obama Girl' now falling out of love," *New York Post,* January 27, 2010.

22.   Young.

23.   Peter Snyder, "Practically Radical" (BIF-5 Collaborative Innovation Summit, Providence, RI, October 7–8, 2009).

CHAPTER 11: EXECUTION IS THE X-FACTOR

1.   Nicolette Robinson, Haruna McWilliams, Felix Bullinger and Clay Schouest, "Dove's Big Ideal: From Real Curves to Growth Curves" (IPA Effectiveness Awards, Institute of Practitioners in Advertising, London, 2008).

2.   Creative Education Foundation, http://www.creativeeducationfoundation.org/?page_id=289 #brainstorming.

3.   Wayne Friedman, "NBCU Airs Integrated Turbo Tax Campaign," *Media Daily News,* January 19, 2010.

4.   Susan Twombly, "Engine Room series from HP & MTV revs up the world's most creative minds," http://www.hp.com/hpinfo/newsroom/feature_stories/2008/08engineroom.html.

5.   Richard Tedesco, "MTV, HP Tool 'Engine Room' for TV and Web," Promomagazine.com, September 12, 2008, http://promomagazine.com/entertainmentmarketing/news/mtv_hp _engine_room_0912/index.html.

6.   Global research study conducted by ZenithOptimedia/MTV.

7.   Ibid.

8.   "Mindshare and Unilever triumph at Valencia Festival of Media Awards," April 21, 2009, http://www.mindshareworld.com/who-we-are/news/@valencia-2009.

9.   Mediacom UK, "Axe Dark Temptation Localisation Strategy," www.creamglobal.com/ search/17798/15546/axe-dark-temptation-localisation-strategy/.

10.   Marisol Bello, "A 'Simpsons' frenzy in Springfield, Vt.," *USA Today,* July 10, 2007.

CHAPTER 12: MEASUREMENT AND METRICS

1.   Light, "Transforming the Marketing Enterprise" (4A Transformation Conference, San Francisco, March 3, 2010).

2.   Harrison, "Effective marketing accountability requires a mix of art and science," *Admap,* June 2009.

3.   Association of National Advertisers, Marketing Accountability Study, April 2008.

4.   Ibid.

5.   "Honomichl Top 50," *Marketing News,* June 30, 2010.

6.   Kevin Clancy, Presentation (Measure Up Conference, Conrad Hilton, Chicago, IL, March 12, 2010).

7.   John Hallward, "'Make Measurable What Is Not So': Consumer Mix Modeling for the Evolving Media World," *Journal of Advertising Research* 48, no. 3 (September 2008): 339–351.

8.   Plummer, Cook, Diforio, Sokolyanskaya and Ovchinnikova, "Measures of Engagement" *Advertising Research Foundation,* White Paper, June 2006.

9.   "Nielsen brings ad engagement research service to UK," February 24, 2010, *Research,* http:// www.research-live.com/news/nielsen-brings-ad-engagement-research-service-to-uk/40021 46.article.

INDEX